WINNING WITH WORDS

WINNING WITH WORDS

Nick Thornely and Dan Lees

MERCURY

First published in 1991
by Mercury Books
Gold Arrow Publications Limited,
862 Garratt Lane, London SW17 0NB

Cartoons by Ken Pyne

Set in Concorde by Phoenix Photosetting

Printed and bound in Great Britain by
Mackays of Chatham PLC, Chatham, Kent

British Library Cataloguing in Publication Data

Thornely, Nick
  Winning with words.
  I. Title   II. Lees, Dan
  808.5

  ISBN 1–85252–083–3

CONTENTS

ACKNOWLEDGEMENTS

The authors wish to thank the following for their help in selecting 'Winning Words' printed at the end of each chapter:

Jeffrey Archer, John Collier, Jilly Cooper, John Crook, Peter Dalton, Lord Charles Forte, Paul Gascoigne, Sir John Harvey-Jones, Sir Denys Henderson, Peter Jackson, Geoffrey Marshall, Dolly Parton, Anita Roddick, Sir Allen Sheppard, Bernard Weatherill, Lord Alexander of Weedon and all the staff at Industrial Motivation Ltd.

INTRODUCTION

For many thousands of years our ancestors believed that words had magical powers – and they were right.

Words can help us to achieve everything we want in life and winning with words can turn our homes into 'comfort zones', improve our social lives and enable us to achieve significant success in the workplace. The power of words belongs to us all – not just to the professionals – and their real magic lies in the fact that they can enable us to win without turning other people into losers. Not only that, but winners with words can usually make the people around them feel like winners as well.

Words can help us to become the sort of 'holistic' winners we talked about in *How to Be a Winner* and *More Ways to Win*, the all-round winners who acquire the habit of winning and of building the people around them into winning teams. Winning is usually better than losing, but wins involving the defeat of other people are often transitory and unsatisfactory, if only because they create enemies. Real winning – based on enlightened self-interest – is almost always permanent and satisfying, even though to the casual observer such wins may seem more like draws.

Some modern philosophers like Arnold Arnold, the author of *Winners and Other Losers in War and Peace*, advocate the draw as the ideal result of most human transactions, pointing out that trying to win in the conventional, competitive sense means treating other people as enemies to be defeated and that this perpetual 'war' results in the breakdown of an increasingly large number of relationships between both individuals and groups.

Arnold argues that the outcome of individual or group gains or losses in this sort of 'zero-sum' society is 'exactly nothing', and he advocates different criteria and a society where there is a net gain for all those individuals and groups who consciously 'play for a draw'.

Mind you, although Arnold's views are valid, neither he nor we would suggest that draws, bargains, negotiated settlements and a winning outcome for everyone are easily achieved in the real world. What we do maintain is that the 'win-win' situation is usually the most desirable outcome and one which the magic of words can help us achieve.

Fortunately, almost all of us are capable of acquiring word magic, a tool so powerful that, while we can use it to help us win in everyday situations, it can also change the fate of nations. However, it can hurt as well as heal and destroy as well as build – which is why winners with words must learn how to control their power.

Of course, we are not suggesting that winning with words involves becoming a demagogue, but the ability to persuade people to follow one's lead can certainly be a winning attribute and using words to motivate a sales team, for instance, is not all that dissimilar to giving a rousing speech to troops who are about to go into battle.

Our ancestors used the power of words to arouse emotions, as well as in many other ways which have their counterparts in the modern world, and long before writing was invented, for example, people used poetry to help them remember seasonal tasks and to pass on information from generation to generation. Nowadays, we store our data on paper or computer disks but we still use the same mnemonic devices as the bards when we make up rhymes or alliterative phrases to help us remember things.

Another memory reinforcer, much favoured by the bards, was repetition – a device still employed today, especially in advertising, and which makes the power of advertising so great that most countries have strict laws to make sure that it is not abused.

In fact, governments have always been chary about letting the power of words get into hands other than their own and, until a few centuries ago, the rulers of England were so afraid of what ordinary people might do if they acquired such power that they transacted all their important business in Latin or French and made it virtually impossible for the peasantry to learn to read and write.

One legacy of this idea that the power of words is 'too dangerous for the common people' is the deliberate obfuscation inherent in the use of jargon and officialese, but at least there is now no question of restricting access to books to administrators and scholars, which makes it doubly sad that there are people who assert – almost as though it were a matter for pride – that they 'never read'. This is equivalent to maintaining that they have nothing to learn from the great writers of the past or present, and we can only assume that such people are victims of an educational policy which habitually confronts young people with works of genius at a time when many of them are still having difficulty with children's comics.

Most winners read a good deal, finding rich and exploitable seams of winning words in books, newspapers and magazines, while even the walking wounded of our educational system are usually able to enjoy good writing when they no longer fear being examined on what they have read. Reading, once we are no longer force-fed on too rich a diet, offers an enjoyable way of acquiring not only winning knowledge but a winning vocabulary and a chance to develop, along correct lines, our individual styles of speaking and writing.

More importantly still, reading should help convince those of us who have English as our mother tongue that, as heirs to what is undoubtedly the most flexible and effective language in the world, we are winners from the first time we begin to speak.

1

WINNING WITH ENGLISH

If you are reading this book the chances are that you are already a winner because anyone who speaks English has drawn a winning ticket in the world's linguistic lottery. As English speakers we can communicate relatively easily with an enormous number of people, while at the same time the language we use – almost without thinking – is the finest linguistic tool in the world and one which not only gives us a flying start in the management of our business and social lives but also puts us well on the way towards winning with words.

DOES ANYBODY HERE SPEAK ENGLISH?

Does anybody here speak English? Ask that question anywhere in the world and you'll almost certainly find someone who can understand you, because more than 750 million people do speak English – over half of them as their mother tongue – while millions more can speak enough of the language to put you on the right road if you are lost or feed you if you're hungry.

Of course, speaking or understanding the same language is no guarantee of instant friendship or a satisfactory conclusion to a business negotiation, but it does help a great deal. In the workplace, for instance, English-speaking businessmen have an obvious advantage in being able to communicate easily with millions of customers, while scientists and engineers can exchange ideas and data in English with colleagues all over the world.

THE LUCK OF THE ENGLISH

There are now more than 2,500 languages in the world so we were extremely fortunate that English became the global language, especially as, when Julius Caesar landed in Britain about 2,000 years ago, the English language did not even exist.

Five hundred years later, as Robert McCrum stresses in *The Story of English*, 'English, incomprehensible to modern ears, was probably spoken by as few people as currently speak Cherokee – and with as little influence.'

By Shakespeare's time, English was still spoken only by some 6 million Englishmen many of whom, because of regional differences, would have had difficulty in understanding each other. That was only around four hundred years ago but, from the time of Elizabeth I, trade followed the flag and England's soldiers, sailors and merchants spread the English language throughout the world.

Of course English had to have a lot more in its favour than courageous fighting men and enterprising traders; after all, the French, the Dutch, the Spaniards and the Portuguese were equally brave and often even more rapacious, but their languages – although spread across vast areas – did not become global communications media in the way English did.

Other countries too were invaded, and in their turn invaded foreign countries, but although this enriched their vocabularies it didn't give them the choice of some 500,000 words which English enjoys – the French, by contrast, have to get by with a mere 100,000 – or make their languages the first choice for international business communications. Romanian, for instance, originally the language of the Roman legionaries, contains so many words from other languages it looks to a foreigner like a dyslexic Esperanto – the Romanian for carp for example is 'crap' – but it was never a contender as an international language.

The fact is that by the time people like Chaucer began writing in English, and Caxton came along to print the works of English writers in their native tongue, English was already a winning tool, ready to serve the genius of Shakespeare and his contemporaries and to advance the cause of English conquest and commerce.

'Give us the tools and we shall finish the job,' said Winston Churchill who, during the Second World War, used words to bring the country back from the brink of defeat.

Like him, as winners with words, we have been given the finest linguistic tool in the world but, had it not been for a series of invasions, a conquest and a winning tendency to find the simplest way out of any difficulty, the language that awaited Shakespeare – and us – might very easily have looked and sounded something like Dutch.

LANGUAGES SHAKEN AND STIRRED

Long before the splendidly effective cocktail called English existed, Britain was populated by the Celts whose descendants now live in Wales, Cornwall, Brittany, Ireland and the Scottish Highlands. They were pushed into those regions by a series of invasions and the Celtic language had relatively little influence on the development of English, although – as if in revenge – the English-speaking Celts of modern times have enriched the language beyond measure.

English itself, after being brought to Britain by invading Germanic tribes, was heavily influenced by Latin and Greek when the country was converted to Christianity by St Augustine – a definite winner with words who described the fair-haired English as 'Not Angles but Angels' – and was later given a strong admixture of Danish by the Vikings. The languages of all the various waves of invaders were Germanic in origin, which meant that they had many words in common and even more that had a familiar ring to them; the trouble was that knowing that a word might mean either 'one horse' or 'two horses' or even 'his horses' was no help when it came to doing business – which of course is what the tribes did as soon as they stopped fighting each other.

What happened then could well have been the most important single factor in making English the business language of the world and it had its curious parallel in a case of linguistic 'revenge' centuries later, when English soldiers fought their way into Schleswig Holstein at the end of the Second World War and discovered that even if they couldn't speak a word of ordinary 'High' German they could understand a lot of the regional dialect, so much so that, in order to trade, the two sides were able to develop a perfectly workable *lingua franca* which was much less complicated than the normal language of either of them.

ENGLISH MADE EASY

Roughly speaking, this is what happened when the various Germanic tribes began talking to each other and discovered that life was a lot easier if, instead of using words with complicated endings, they used the basic word for, say, 'horse', plus a couple of smaller words to determine how many horses, whose horse or horses and what was being done to or by the animals in question.

In this way they not only added to their vocabularies – by, say, retaining the original word for horse in one language to denote a particular kind of horse – but, much more importantly, got rid of a great deal of the grammatical baggage which bedevils so many other languages, making them difficult to learn and often unwieldy to use. The vast debt we owe to the Vikings and the rest of the Nordic invaders who were too idle or too crafty to bother learning the troublesome complexities of each other's languages is easily appreciated by anyone who has had to learn all the German words for 'the', only to discover that the nouns, too, change their endings according to circumstances as do almost all other parts of speech. In addition, German – like French and many other languages – is saddled with a totally illogical system of gender in which, in the case of German, every noun is either masculine, feminine or neuter which makes German, as Mark Twain put it, 'a language in which a young lady has no sex but a turnip has'.

This simplification process made English a relatively easy language for foreigners to learn, or at least to understand, and an ideal basis for 'pidgin', or business language, which ultimately helped the British and Americans to spread their commercial empires throughout the world. It still has this virtue of being easy to learn as a basic tool of communication, but in revenge many of the factors which helped make it simple – in the form of an 800-word vocabulary of basic English – also made it so flexible and so full of nuances that it is difficult to speak well and virtually impossible to speak perfectly.

Unfortunately, at the same time, the deceptive simplicity of English leads many of us to believe that – unlike Germans who have to learn to speak good German or the French who must learn to speak good French – we are able to speak and write excellent English without bothering to give the language a great deal of thought.

This is not a winning attitude for a people with a simple language which is paradoxically so complicated as to be two languages for the price of one – a situation for which we must blame the French and specifically William the Conqueror.

1066 – AND ALL THAT 'EMBARRAS DE RICHESSE'

The Danes and the rest of the Germanic invaders added richness to the English vocabulary but it was the arrival of the Norman French which gave us what amounted to a parallel language, so that our winning language of today has a 'loud' pedal and a 'soft' pedal, a blunt plain speaking mode and a polite, courtly, scholarly mode – a doubly effective language the advantages of which, in business and other negotiations, can hardly be overestimated.

These twin streams of English eventually merged into a winning language of incomparable, almost embarrassing richness but this didn't happen overnight and it was the 'apartheid' in linguistic matters, imposed by the Normans and enthusiastically embraced by their English collaborators, which allowed English to develop as a winning language and enables us to shift conversational gears at will, whether we are negotiating, selling or making love.

One illustration of the dual nature of English is the fact

that, unlike most other languages, we still use different words for live animals and their meat, because after the Conquest the English peasantry, who didn't get to eat much meat, called the animals by their Anglo-Saxon names – giving us such words as cow, sheep, pig and so on – while the Normans, who were used to seeing meat on their trenchers, or '*tranches*', of bread, gave us the French-derived names of beef (*boeuf*), mutton (*mouton*) and pork (*porc*).

IT MAY BE A COW DOWN HERE, AEGBURT, BUT UP THERE IT'S THE ROAST BOEUF OF OLD NORMANDY

Incidentally, as well as making English an immensely flexible winning language, this linguistic apartheid left a legacy of subtle language snobbery – remember U and non-U? – which winners with words should at least be able to recognise for what it is and perhaps even make use of.

PRACTICAL WINNING

Pick a couple of sentences, one plain and straightforward and the other a little flowery, and decide in both cases which words you either know or suspect are of Anglo-Saxon origin and those more likely to be derived from the French, checking your results with any dictionary large enough to give derivations.

It may help to remember that Winston Churchill's famous speech about fighting 'on the beaches' contains only one word derived from the French – a choice which, in the circumstances, was perhaps politically motivated, since it was the word 'surrender'.

TO THINK OR NOT TO THINK?

Making conscious decisions about our language and vocabulary, which is essential if we are to win with words, might seem at first to be as awkward as thinking about every move we make while learning to drive or working on our golf swing. In the end, however, it is surprisingly easy to switch back to 'automatic', selecting the mood of our communication and letting our built-in computer do much of the rest – so easy in fact that, as with many other accomplishments, once mastered it is hard to understand what made it seem difficult in the first place.

WINNING IN PRINT

The extent and duration of Norman linguistic apartheid can be judged by the fact that it was more than 350 years after the Conquest before Henry V became the first king of England to use English for his official correspondence, a lead which the ordinary people were quick to follow. It was this that enabled Caxton to print the works of Chaucer and others in English – something of a mixed blessing, as it happened, since he fixed the spelling of words as he heard them in south-east England and before a 'national' pronunciation had been decided on, which accounts for many of the idiosyncracies of our English spelling. Winners with words who are not completely happy with the orthography of their mother tongue at least have an interesting excuse.

ENGLISH TAKES OFF

Fuelled by the sheer energy of the Elizabethan Age, English really took off as a world language and was revelled in by Shakespeare and his contemporaries who were enthralled by its richness and power and who, in turn, added to its splendours. From then on it went from strength to strength, not only spreading throughout the world as the common languages of millions who would never see its country of origin, but gathering new words from every conceivable language and adding them to the hundreds of thousands of words in its vocabulary.

And as English soldiers, adventurers and traders took over and adapted words from Dutch, Spanish, German, Flemish, Danish, Swedish – not to mention Hebrew,

Arabic, Hindi, Chinese, Malay and the rest – both they and the stay-at-homes were immersing themselves in the language of the Bible which was one of the few books most ordinary folk possessed. The end result of the whole process was an unstoppable triumph for the English language which has become the language of international business, the language of the sea, the language of the air and the language of the new technology.

THE ENGLISH LANGUAGES

'Britain and America', the saying goes, 'are two countries divided by a common language,' but in fact the division operates, at least nowadays, in only one direction, which means that while some Americans may experience difficulty in understanding 'English' English, there can be few British people who don't understand a great deal of 'American'. Perhaps the most important reason for this is the large number of American films and television programmes which most Britons see – and listen to; a one-way linguistic 'immersion' which enables them to pick up American by osmosis.

Another reason for the largely unidirectional linguistic traffic is that while the Americans have regional accents, speech patterns and vocabularies, they do not have dialects. Thus, while Americans have little difficulty in understanding other Americans, they find English regional speech confusing. This was not always the case and before the War of American Independence the English of the two countries was very similar, although the English had already begun to complain about 'Americanisms' and the American 'dialect'. In fact, the saying to the effect that 'a language is a dialect with an army and navy' might very well have been coined to fit the American revolutionaries, who were the first to begin talking about an American language and in some cases would have liked to have rid themselves of the hated British connection altogether. So bitter were some Americans that French was seriously put forward as a language for the new nation because it would annoy the British, while other extreme nationalists advocated the adoption of Greek or Hebrew.

Fortunately for English speakers, most of the leaders of the American Revolution – while totally in favour of American English – realised that English itself had too strong a hold to be deposed. As John Adams wrote in 1780, 'English is destined to be in the next and succeeding centuries more generally the language of the world than Latin was in the last or French is in the present age. The reason for this is obvious, because the increasing population in America, and their universal connections and correspondence with other nations will, aided by the influence of England in the world, whether great or small, force their language into general use.'

Adams was right, English – American or otherwise – was destined to be the world language of the future and Thomas Jefferson, who had proved himself a winner with words by drafting most of the splendidly stirring Declaration of Independence, saw even more clearly what would be the main thrust behind the American version of the language. 'Judicious neology', he wrote, 'can alone give strength and copiousness to language, and enable it to be the vehicle of new ideas.'

In the end it was not only neologisms – inventions like Jefferson's own 'belittle' and the vocabulary of twentieth-century technology – that gave American English vitality and richness, but the waves of immigrant Germans,

Russians, Poles, Italians, French and the Yiddish – literally Jud Deutsch, or Jewish German – speaking Jews.

Cowboys, crooks, entertainers and the rest all contributed to the language that swept back across the Atlantic and – although at first the defenders of English English rejected these new riches – nowadays even many of the purists concede that, after being subjected to the triage of common usage, the American imports add freshness and life to the English language.

Meanwhile much the same process has added yet more words and phrases from Australia, Canada, South Africa and the rest of the English-speaking world, many of which – like the American contributions – are shared by all, ensuring that the language wherever it is spoken is constantly updated and revitalised.

All these factors make English the ideal language with which to win with words and to face up to today's challenges and opportunities, but unfortunately not all of us realise just how lucky we are.

SO WHAT WENT WRONG?

Sadly, due partly to bad teaching and partly to our insular feelings of superiority, not all English speakers appreciate their good fortune. They not only speak and write badly but their communication skills are so sloppy that they frequently convey only an approximation of their intended message and even, on occasions, say or write the exact opposite to what they mean. It's rather as if, having been presented with a magnificent pipe organ, all they can manage to play is an inaccurate version of 'Chopsticks', a state of affairs made worse by the fact that some of them even boast of their lack of communication skills.

Winners, on the other hand, know that they have inheri-
ted a language so flexible it can change from a bludgeon to
an epée – or for that matter to a magic wand – in a matter of
seconds, a language that they can use to help them win
whatever they want from life.

WINNING WITH MORE WORDS

Most winners have been winning with words to a certain
extent all their lives and, unlike losers who affect to despise
even the ability to write a decent letter, winners know that
word skills are not only essential but can always be
developed and improved upon. A good vocabulary, for
example, is a must if we wish to win with words, but
unfortunately even the word 'vocabulary' itself has been
ruined by the schoolroom where, for most of us, it picked
up the association of long lists of foreign words and the
inevitable 'tests'. Incidentally, the word for vocabulary in
German is *Wortschatz*, or 'word treasure', which gives a
much better idea of the delights in store for those of us who
like to play around with the dictionary – sadly another
word which reeks of the schoolroom.

The *Reader's Digest* runs a feature called 'It Pays to
Improve Your Word Power' and the use of the word
'power' is interesting. Our way of improving our word
power is to look up in the dictionary any word which
refuses to yield its meaning from its context or of which we
need to check the spelling. Mind you, it often takes us at
least half an hour to look up a word like 'appetite' because
we then come across something like 'alchemy' and discover
that its root is Arabic and that the 'al' simply means 'the' –
which gives us a whole new slant on words like algebra,

alcohol, alambic and alhambra and the influence of Arabic culture on Western life.

We should confess that meandering through the dictionary in this way can seriously endanger your timetable but on the other hand it will help give you a winning vocabulary, besides turning you into a wellnigh unbeatable Scrabble player.

To get the most out of the dictionary as a winning aid you should get hold of one like the *Concise Oxford* or *Collins* which are large enough to contain not only definitions of words but examples of how they are used, together with their derivations.

WINNERS AREN'T SESQUIPEDALIAN

Most of us who make a conscious effort to enlarge our vocabulary tend in the first instance to become a little sesquipedalian – a glorious word with its own built-in irony, meaning 'a tendency to use long words merely to impress'. This is not all that serious, as long as it doesn't last too long, and winners usually find that within a short time they are selecting precisely the right word, whether long or short, an essential skill if we are to win with words and especially if we are to become winning conversationalists, which is one important way of getting what we want.

PRACTICAL WINNING

Look up in any reasonably comprehensive dictionary the first word that comes into your head, taking care to look at the words at the head of each page as you flick through. If you start looking up some of the odd words you come across in this way, instead of the one you set out to find, you stand a very good chance indeed of becoming even more of a winner with words than you are at the moment. You could also check a couple of recent letters in your files for evidence of sesquipedalianism and translate some of the needlessly lengthy words into more everyday speech – a useful exercise, especially if the letters are ones you wrote yourself.

Winning Words

The heights by great men reached and kept,
Were not attained by sudden flight,
But they, while their companions slept,
Were toiling upward in the night.
  Henry Wadsworth Longfellow

A wise man blames himself.
A fool blames others.
  Confucius

Life is like riding a bicycle. If you stop pedalling you can freewheel for a while – but eventually you will fall off!

2

WINNING THE CONVERSATION GAME

The use of language is the best way we human beings have of getting what we want and, as we have seen, English with its splendid mixture of simplicity and subtlety is the finest available linguistic tool. This means that English speakers enjoy a great advantage when it comes to winning with words, the importance of which can be judged by the fact that every time we open our mouths to speak or use words to communicate we do so because we want something.

At first sight this may seem a cynical viewpoint but in reality the variety of human wishes is such that our wants cover an infinite range of desires from the saintly and altruistic to the evil and selfish and 'wanting something' is an integral part of the human condition.

In fact, the realisation that all of us who use words want something is essential if we are to win with words as it helps us to decide what we ourselves want and also to ask ourselves what other people want from us, without automatically suspecting that they intend to harm us. This means that, once we accept that other people's wants are not necessarily inimical to our own, we should find it easier to perceive, for example, sales presentations and negotiations of all types as co-operative rather than adversarial situations.

For winners with words, phrases like 'What does he want?' or 'I wonder what she's after?' do not necessarily imply cynicism or suspicion. We know that if people are talking to us they want something, even if it is only a chat, and it is up to us to find out if we can satisfy their wants while at the same time satisfying our own.

This means that if we are to win with words we must struggle against any xenophobic feelings we may have, whether inborn or acquired, and become more outgoing and more generous with strangers. One of the best ways to do this is to practise the art of conversation because, in addition to helping us overcome any fear of strangers, conversation can enable us to develop the skills we need to win with words in more formal situations.

Unfortunately the very word 'conversation' dismays some people as it conjures up nightmares in which they are the helpless target of rapier-tongued and malicious wits. It shouldn't, of course, partly because the supply of rapier-tongued wits – malicious or otherwise – is sadly limited and partly because conversation simply means 'the interchange through speech of information, ideas, etc.' – in other words, talking to people.

Looking up words in the dictionary, as well as being a useful and interesting exercise, can often take the sting out of them. It is difficult to be too worried about conversation, for example, when we discover that 'criminal conversation' used to mean adultery.

For our purposes conversation simply means talking to people because, after all, communication is what winning with words is all about, and knowing how to talk to people makes all the difference when it comes to handling our-selves at the negotiating table, selling our ideas or products, or, for that matter, speaking to a hall full of people or broadcasting to millions.

RELAX – WE'RE ONLY TALKING

Of course we still want something, even if we are only chatting. Conversation, as well as providing us with enjoyment, can help us to make friends, to discover new relationships, to elicit useful information, to extend our network of allies and a great deal more. However, unlike more formal discussions, it is not normally recorded – which means that we have a chance to practise our word skills without pressure and that, unless we have some particularly litigious or treacherous friends, we are unlikely to finish up defending our position in court or in front of a board meeting.

ANYONE CAN TALK – OR CAN THEY?

Not many people would maintain that 'anyone' can pilot a jet plane, or for that matter play a decent game of golf, but there would be plenty prepared to defend the proposition that 'anyone' can talk.

The fact is that the range of human verbal prowess ranges from the ability to make barely intelligible noises to the rarefied wit of the Senior Common Room and the coruscating repartee of a Sir Peter Ustinov or, for that matter, a Dame Edna Everidge.

Winners realise that, while some people seem blessed with more innate verbal skills than others, it is possible for most of us to increase our conversational ability – in other words, anyone can learn to talk. They also realise that the only way to take part in a conversation is to say something and that this activity, as is plain from the dictionary definition, involves an 'interchange' of ideas. Conversation implies an unspoken and informal contract like those implicit in many communication situations, and without this contract to exchange information and ideas a conversation becomes a harangue, a one-sided affair, as unsatisfactory as a game of tennis with no rallies.

WINNERS OPEN THEIR MOUTHS

It sounds simplistic to the point of idiocy but one good way to start a conversation is to say something to somebody.

Not everyone seems to realise this and one often hears people say things like: 'They were dreadfully snobbish. They didn't say a word to us all night,' only to discover that the person doing the complaining didn't open his mouth once in the course of the evening, not even to say 'Hello!'

If we are to improve our conversational skills, we must expose ourselves to the danger of becoming involved in conversation, which means talking to the people in our homes, in the house next door, in the pub, in the workplace – in fact anywhere.

WINNING BEGINS AT HOME

One of the best places to begin winning with words is the home. It's the logical place to start the ripple effect which begins with our change of attitude to words and language and spreads steadily outwards as we become winners with family, friends and colleagues.

It's a good place to start learning to win with words, because in most cases the people with whom we share our home will be tolerant and helpful and also because – unless our family life is totally horrendous – we will normally be forced into regular verbal encounters, even if only of the 'Pass the butter' kind, which at least gives us something to build on.

Those of us who are fortunate enough to have homes which are already comfort zones, where all the family feel 'happy in their skins' and where light-hearted verbal jousting and laughter are the norm, have a head start when it comes to winning with words.

Meanwhile, those whose homes are cold comfort zones have a great deal of polite, patient persisting to do if they are to change the climate.

SILENCE IS NOT GOLDEN

One of the worst situations to be found in any family or group is when some or all of its members 'aren't talking' – by which we don't mean that they are sulking or taking a little private time but that they are literally not exchanging a single word. Shouting is bad enough but it is at least a form of communication and holds a promise that things may improve. The sort of silence we are talking about lasts until silence itself becomes a weapon in a fight to the death.

Of course winners will attempt to break the silence before it reaches this stage but, in the rare cases when things become as bad as this, the winning move could well be to leave.

If they are able to begin talking again, they may find themselves at the very basic communication level of those families who grunt, snarl and generally exchange signals rather than hold civilised conversations, in which case they may well discover that the next step is to try talking at mealtimes when there is less likely to be competition from the TV. To avoid arguments in the initial stages, try talking at the breakfast table – even if it means getting up a few minutes earlier than usual. Begin with trivia, working up from 'pass the butter' to the weather, going on to minor family concerns and bearing in mind that all human beings, with the possible exception of saints, are primarily concerned with themselves and their own interests.

'How's your cold – did you manage to get some sleep?' is much more likely to be the start of a winning conversation then 'My God! I didn't sleep a wink last night,' while the previous evening's TV can often be a useful starter, especially as it will usually reflect the interests of the person concerned.

WINNERS AND LOSERS

Fortunately, complete silence of the 'not speaking' kind is rare, and, in most communication situations, while there's talk there's hope.

A far more common 'losing' state is one in which people are sniping at each other, becoming steadily more vicious as they try to score points in a marathon verbal battle.

This, curiously enough, is quite close to the way in which the family situation can be used as a training ground for discussion and debate in the workplace and elsewhere, and all that is required is an appreciation of the fact that winners do *not* win by making other people lose, but by arranging things so that everyone wins – which for some people involves changing the conversational habits of a lifetime by, for example, ceasing to beat their children.

STOP BEATING YOUR CHILDREN!

Of course, you don't really beat your children – or your spouse – but you may, unwittingly, cause them consider-able pain by your use of words, especially if you find yourself frustrated in the workplace and take it out on the soft targets within the family.

Words are magic but it's a magic which when wrongly employed, as in the case of adults using biting sarcasm against young children, can not only be devastating but can cause permanent damage.

In the home, perhaps even more than anywhere else, winners make their immediate surroundings into a conver-sational comfort zone for the whole group, but this doesn't mean that all conversations within the family have to be banal, colourless or even completely amicable.

In fact, the home is the ideal place for winners to sharpen their conversational claws but while doing so they can perhaps learn from the animals. Most animals learn to defend themselves by indulging in 'play' fights and, although these can become fierce as the combatants become stronger and more experienced, few animals are seriously hurt.

Winners try to make sure that in any verbal fencing the partners are evenly matched, that no one takes advantage of superior skill and experience and that, as is the case with animals, everyone knows when to stop.

Some animals signal that they wish to surrender by rolling over on their backs or showing their bottoms. While this could be fun, it might cause comment so, in most winning families, sparring partners have verbal signals or codes which indicate when things are becoming too serious. In one family we know, the wife's accent changes fractionally towards that of her native county when she is really annoyed – a signal for her husband or other family members to stop teasing her.

PRACTICAL WINNING

If – and only if – you have the sort of family you know will help, even if they begin by teasing you, enlist their aid by asking them to identify any conversational bad habits you may have. This might sound something of a masochistic way in which to begin winning with words, but if it works you will have made tremendous strides because wins are cumulative and eliminating bad habits in the home helps us to avoid them in the workplace and elsewhere.

We may, for instance, discover to our horror that we

have a tendency to be overly sarcastic or pompous, that we tend to switch off – while still seeming to listen – or that we jump in with interruptions when other people are speaking, all bad enough at home but definite Loserspeak elsewhere, especially in the workplace.

Mind you, we are not saying that winners never interrupt – they are not saints after all and they do sometimes lose patience with mumblers, bumblers and those who are wrong-headed enough to disagree with them – they just try not to make a habit of it.

TIMING IS ALL

Judging when to begin speaking is a question of timing, one of the most important verbal skills, and if your children tell you, for example, 'You're always interrupting' there is every chance that you may be doing the same thing in the pub or in the workplace.

In this, as in so many other situations, enlightened self-interest should persuade us to improve our timing because winners know that if they continually jump in with interruptions, they may miss something important and eventually people may stop trying to tell them things altogether.

Winning conversations in the home, as much as elsewhere, should be based on good manners and the golden rule of 'Do As You Would Be Done By.' This doesn't mean that winners shouldn't have fun trying to cap each other's lines – which after all is half the joy of many conversations – but it does mean that family conversations should be friendly exchanges rather than verbal battles which invariably leave one party staggering from the field in tears.

Timing is the basis of good situation comedy so it's worth

watching some of the better examples of verbal jousting on TV, taking particular notice of the timing and the way in which – in the better examples – words are used to score 'laughter points' rather than to score off other people.

Of course the TV shows have been scripted, polished and rehearsed before being recorded, so we shouldn't be too worried if we don't reach a similar standard; but, on the other hand, most families have a lot of good material to work with and in some cases have been behaving like an informal repertory company for years.

WINNERS REHEARSE

Of course there is no need to rehearse family conversations – although there could be a case for winners giving careful thought to the way they would like to see more serious discussions develop – but the family is a good place to acquire this useful skill.

Winners should remember that rehearsing is different from worrying and that the former will, in fact, help to reduce the pressures inherent in many social or business situations.

When experimenting with rehearsals in the family context we could, for example, decide on the topic of conversation we are going to introduce, mentally running through the other participants and their characters, their likes and dislikes and so on, so that we can, perhaps, decide in advance whether to use a 'hard' or 'soft' mode – straightforward Anglo-Saxon or more polite and more circuitous Norman-French.

Naturally there's no way we can guess exactly what the other participants in the conversation will say in reply to our lines but what we do, in effect, is compose a series of playlets in our minds in which the dialogue may take several different turns – the secret, incidentally, of many actors' ability to improvise. None of these will be precisely the same as in the real conversation but they may be sufficiently like it to give us the advantage and enable us to win. For this reason, learning how to exercise partial control over the way conversations and discussions develop by rehearsing them in advance is invaluable preparation for the times when the discussions become more serious.

PRACTICAL WINNING

Words like 'invaluable', which look as though they could easily mean the exact opposite, make most of us think twice, and it's worthwhile opening a notebook in which to make a record of words of this sort, along with any new, interesting or troublesome ones and any words which strike us as 'winners'. Keep a note, too, of any derivations you find particularly interesting as they may occasionally provide useful material for use in general conversation.

WINNING WITH WORDS IN THE PUB

Pubs are splendid places in which to practise and enjoy the art of conversation and we ourselves have been known to visit the odd hostelry in order to brush up our conversational skills. In fact – and brewers should send a donation in cash or in kind via our publishers – there is no better place to learn how to win with words than a really good pub in which people can mix without shyness, and without the inhibitions and restrictions imposed elsewhere by education, status and class.

In a good pub we should find all the types we are likely to meet when taking part in more serious discussions and negotiations but in a relaxed, outgoing and holiday humour.

A good pub is an ideal example of a conversational comfort zone and the good publican or barman is like a benign chairman, seeking to put everyone at their ease and introducing strangers into congenial company. Of course, the best of landlords know that winning with words in this way will help them to sell more ale but the customers become winners too in yet another unspoken contract – in this case to provide more than beer in exchange for money.

In their search for good pubs and good conversation, winners should try every class of bar from four ale to cocktail – an exercise which will help them to become conversational chameleons who can subtly alter their accent and vocabulary without stooping to conscious imitation. This can pay enormous dividends in the workplace and elsewhere as well as providing a good excuse to seek out some decent ale.

The pub is a great place for winners to discover, if need be, that not all chaps in cloth caps are illiterate oafs and that, by the same token, not everyone with a plummy accent and an old school tie is a complete snob. It's also a place where we can learn respect for our conversational partners which will stand us in good stead for a lifetime of discussions, whatever position we may achieve.

Incidentally, with a bit of luck, we could also learn how to deal with the occasional awkward customer – like the conversational bully – which is all good practice for dealing with such people on other social occasions or at work.

Sadly, women for the most part are deprived of the

opportunity to make full use of pubs as places in which to win with words, as in many cases it is impossible for them either to go into bars on their own or, if they do so, to initiate conversations. However, they can make up for this at parties and other social occasions.

WINNING AT PARTIES

Ordinary parties, as opposed to business receptions, are also good places in which to learn and practise conversational skills under conditions in which any mistakes we make won't normally have any serious repercussions.

Guests at parties are perhaps more likely to form homogeneous groups with common interests than are the customers of most pubs, but joining in or even initiating conversations at parties should hold few terrors for the accomplished pub conversationalist. Winners should not be afraid to talk to people they haven't met before; they should try to make a genuine contribution, listen to what other people have to say and refrain from either jumping in or switching off. Above all, they should not trust to alcohol either to relieve any boredom they may feel or to increase their conversational brilliance. In many ways if you're not fit to drive you're not fit to talk, but strict application of this rule would have deprived the world of some wonderful conversations so it's up to winners to find their own level of stimulation.

Here again, ordinary parties – like pubs – are the places where we can learn how to handle alcohol and words together, whereas receptions and formal dinner parties are not, while teetotallers and wine bibbers should make allowances for the fact that they tend to shine at different ends of any given social gathering.

WINNING AT DINNER PARTIES

All the suggestions for winning with words we have talked about so far apply to dinner parties, but for these more formal occasions a little intelligence work is in order – especially if the dinner is connected with the workplace. Winners may find it useful, for instance, to know about the jobs, interests, political persuasions, hobbies and so on of their hosts and, if possible, some of the other guests. Of course, nobody would expect you to become an expert on any particular subject in a couple of days but if, for example, a guest mentions at table that he's keen on apiculture it could help if you have found out in advance that his hobby is keeping bees.

Winning hosts of course make every effort to make their dinner table into a comfort zone, especially if their guests happen to be lower down the company ladder.

At a good dinner party, perhaps more than most conversational situations, practised winners will change conversational gears until they know the people they are talking to feel comfortable. We have one journalist friend who remembers talking about economics with Sir Harold Wilson and confesses ruefully that when the then Prime Minister judged he had reached the appropriate intellectual level he still seemed to have several gears in hand.

WINNING AT BUSINESS RECEPTIONS

Apart from the office Christmas party – which is best followed by general and total amnesia – business receptions and firms' social gatherings are occasions at which winners with words can expect to shine. At such affairs, winners are conscious of the fact that they may have bosses but do not have superiors and that while they may have subordinates or assistants they do not have inferiors. This means that, while they may vary their accent and speech patterns slightly, depending on who they are talking to, they will not talk down to some people or be subservient to others.

As is the case with all types of verbal encounter, winners – although essentially quick-thinking opportunists – will have given some thought to the type of reception they are to attend and will have identified their aims.

They will have decided in advance what it is they want and whether they expect an enjoyable exchange of small talk, a chance to make new contacts or the opportunity to do some low-key intelligence gathering. Winners with words, of course, will be able to do all these things and more, while being manifestly pleasant and intelligent individuals who know how to listen to and appreciate other people's points of view. At the same time they may well have placed a tentative foot on the next rung of the promotion ladder and, if unattached, may even leave the function with someone devastatingly attractive, potentially useful, or both – all of which is what makes being a winner with words worth the effort.

GOLDEN RULE

A golden rule of conversation is to remember that most human beings, whatever their age, race, creed or social status, are convinced that they are the most fascinating creatures on earth and that their activities, relationships, politics, illnesses, etc., past, present and future, are the only topics of conversation which are of any real interest.

Winning Words

A gossip is one who talks to you about others; a bore is one who talks to you about himself; and a brilliant conversationalist is one who talks to you about *your*self!
 Lisa Kirk

I hear – I forget
I see – I remember
I do – I understand
 Confucius

Humour is the life jacket in the River of Life.
 W Raabe

3

JUST A FEW
WINNING WORDS

Invite a winner to 'say a few words' and he'll almost certainly be happy to oblige because, unlike those timorous creatures who would rather face a cage full of tigers than an audience, he knows that an opportunity to speak in public gives most of us one of the best chances of winning with words we are likely to get.

After all, what other occasion enables us to speak to several people – or several hundred – for ten minutes or more with very little fear of interruption? What other occasion practically guarantees us a friendly hearing, with listeners who can be presumed to have at least a minimal interest in what we have to say and who are held captive by their own good manners until we choose to stop talking?

Unless an audience is hostile from the outset – which is highly unlikely on either social or business occasions – these are ideal conditions in which to win with words and a splendid training ground for situations in which the speaker holds fewer advantages.

A WINNING SPEECH IS A WINNING CONVERSATION

A public speech which invites questions from the audience is a 'conversation' in which the speaker is given not only the massive advantage of having first go, but usually the lion's share of the time available. It is also a conversation in which the speaker is formally invited to make his best and most important points, having been given adequate time to marshal his thoughts, to write them down, to rehearse them and to anticipate any points or counter-arguments which may be put to him after he's finished speaking.

This of course is where the winner's increasingly wide-ranging reading, his interest in words in general and the English language in particular – together with his practice in initiating and directing conversations at home, in social situations and in the workplace – begin to pay additional dividends, enabling him to win with words yet again.

WHEN WINNERS MAKE A SPEECH THERE ARE NO LOSERS

At first sight, speaking in public seems to be a situation so heavily weighted in favour of the speaker that, whatever he does, he must finish up a winner, having imposed his thoughts and opinions on his captive and defenceless audience at will.

In reality, however, if we are to win with words we must recognise that here again is an implied contract, an undertaking that in return for the audience giving us an uninterrupted hearing and sympathetic attention, we as speakers are required to be informative or amusing and ideally both. As speakers it is we who set the tone and, whether we are speaking to a handful of relatives or broadcasting to the nation, our aim should be to turn everywhere within range of our voice into a comfort zone in which everyone listening feels at ease.

This is not to say that all public speeches must necessarily be anodyne or neutral – in fact the warmer the comfort zone, the more effective will be the occasional shocking or provocative words – but in almost every case the aim of the speaker, no matter how heartfelt his arguments, should be to provoke thought, discussion and eventually harmony, rather than the sort of riot to which the police have to be called.

Winners ask themselves 'what do I want?' and keep the purpose of their speech firmly in mind while preparing and making it – otherwise it's all too easy to be carried away by one's own enthusiasm and to ride a hobby horse right out of the hall. But whether they are proposing a toast or making a political broadcast their object is to inform, to entertain and to persuade, so that after a winning speech everyone goes home happy – especially the speaker. It can be so easy that winners find it difficult to understand why many people find the prospect of opening their mouths in public so terrifying.

IF IT'S ALL SO EASY WHY ARE MY KNEES SHAKING?

At this point we're not talking about professional politicians, or for that matter the stars of stage, screen and golf club, although even many of them would confess to a touch of nerves immediately before they go on.

This is the body's natural response to 'flee or fight' situations which demand peak performance – adrenalin flows, blood pumps and waste disposal systems prepare the body for fast movement by ridding it of excess weight – and if it helped our prehistoric ancestors to escape from sabre-toothed tigers and the like, it can certainly hype us up to the point where we are able to win with words.

Unfortunately some of these reactions are unwelcome when our intention is to make a speech rather than fight for our lives or flee across the savannah, but they can be countered by breathing deeply, forcing air into the diaphragm and then expelling it with some vigour which, as many sportsmen and martial arts experts appreciate, also increases one's energy.

Winners learn to recognise and appreciate the mind-concentrating touch of nerves or stage fright before they begin to speak in public, but no one would wish to experience the feeling of terror that affects many people when they are asked to address an audience – a stomach-churning fear quite different from the feelings which should help to put speakers into a 'readiness' mode.

LOSING EXPECTATIONS

There are two main non-physical reasons for the irrational fears some people feel when asked to 'say a few words', one of which is the fear of ridicule and a desire to keep a low profile, which could well date back to the time when people who were in any way different were frequently killed out of hand.

The other is the fact that fear of public speaking, like our fear of dentists, has become part of our folklore, so that in both cases, while we know that it is in the highest degree unlikely that anything really bad will happen, we have been told so often that 'everyone' is frightened, that it becomes a self-fulfilling prophecy.

Winners can deal with these groundless but none the less real fears by using the Worst Possible Scenario – usually a planning technique. They simply ask what is the very worst thing that could happen should they fail to make a winning speech? Will they be dragged from the hall and hanged, drawn and quartered or subjected to other unspeakable tortures? Unlikely; it's tough to get qualified help for that sort of work these days.

Will they – having failed to hold the attention of their listeners – be pelted with rotten fruit? Again unlikely; unless the audience suspect in advance that they might need such missiles, which are otherwise difficult to get hold of at the drop of a platitude.

Verbal barracking and abuse? The sack? Social ostracism? No; in most cases the worst that could happen would be a distinct feeling of inadequacy and some murmurs of disapproval and half-hearted applause rather than a standing ovation. Winners know they could live with anything of this sort – but are confident that they won't have to.

WINNERS FULFIL THE PUBLIC SPEAKER'S CONTRACT

Professional after-dinner speakers, who command large fees for talking in public, know that once they have agreed to speak for a cash payment there is an actual or implied contract which requires them to give value for money.

Winners know that the amateur speaker, called upon to talk to the Chamber of Commerce or the Women's Institute, has also made an implied contract to give value in exchange for a few drinks and a decent lunch, or even merely for the courtesy of a hearing. The apprehension some people experience on being invited to speak in public is due to a very real fear that they may not be able to keep their side of the bargain, whereas winners, having prepared in advance, know they are going to be good value.

WINNERS PREPARE FOR THE UNEXPECTED

On the principle of 'train hard – fight easy', winners do their homework when they know they are to speak in public but there is no way one can be totally prepared for the well meaning idiot who bangs his glass with a spoon at the end of a decent meal and announces, without warning: 'And now, ladies and gentlemen, I'm sure we'll all be very interested to hear a few words from Joe Muggins.'

Winning move number one – apart from hissing to the proposer of this unscheduled entertainment that you will get him if it's the last thing you do – is to institute some sort of delaying tactic, which can range from a fit of coughing to spilling a glass of wine, preferably into the lap of the person who asked you to speak without warning.

It's astonishing how long it takes to mumble an apology, to gaze around helplessly for someone with enough gumption to hand the victim a napkin and so on. Abraham Lincoln would probably have found it sufficient breathing space in which to think up the Gettysburg address. All you have to do is 'say a few words'.

Mind you, winners will never be totally unprepared for

such situations. Suspecting that they may one day be asked to speak without prior notice, they will have a few all-purpose words up their sleeve, including the odd joke about being caught unawares, which gives them more thinking time and also makes sure everyone present *knows* they were caught unawares. 'Well, ladies and gentlemen, as I'm sure you'll appreciate, after that little contretemps – I was caught entirely unaware, but as the great Groucho Marx once said, "Who cares as long as your unnerwear's clean?" . . .'

PRACTICAL WINNING

Think up half a dozen delaying tactics and incorporate each of them into an introduction that will let people know that you were caught unprepared; for example, 'I'm sorry about that fit of coughing. Of course, if I know I'm going to be asked to speak I never travel without a ton of cough sweets, a gallon of linctus and a vet, but unfortunately this evening . . .'

Imagine a few situations in which you might be asked to speak without notice, like a wedding reception or a colleague's retirement, and think up a short speech you might give. Think of your performance in terms of blocks, i.e. delaying tactic, introduction, body of speech, conclusion; then, when you *are* asked to speak, all you have to do is to change a few details and you have a cracking 'off-the-cuff' speech. Keep plenty of snappy quotes and one-liners available by writing them down whenever you come across them and don't worry too much if you can't remember exactly who said what, provided you don't claim the credit for yourself. After all, as Disraeli remarked on one occasion, 'A quote is a quote is a quote.' Record your all-purpose speech on tape for polishing, future reference and timing as soon as you are happy with it – and *remember to keep it short*.

HOW MANY IS A FEW?

As far as winning speeches, especially impromptu ones, are concerned, a 'few' words means exactly that. At three words a second or 180 words a minute – particularly if you are not being paid for them – five minutes or 900 words, which is the length of a decent-sized newspaper feature article, should be enough for most social occasions. Unless there are very special circumstances, winners who are asked to speak for longer than five minutes, without being given adequate time for preparation, should decline to do so.

A QUESTION OF WINNING

Once winners are confident that they can make a short off-the-cuff speech at any time, one for which they are able to prepare is a piece of wedding cake.

First you need some information from your hosts and – if you are going to be asked to speak in public on a regular basis – it's as well to prepare an all-purpose questionnaire, so that all you have to do is fill in the details each time, or better still have someone fill them in for you.

Things winners *must* know include:

- Where is the speech to be given? Exact address, with details on how to get there.

- What is the speech to be about and how long?

- How many people are expected?

- Correct names, titles and positions of all VIPs.

- What sort of public address system is there, if any?

- Are they the main speaker and, if not, where do they come in the batting order? Who are the others – and, particularly, who is speaking before them?

Unless they are being paid a decent fee, and perhaps even then, winners should expect the secretary of the host organisation to complete this questionnaire and to provide any other relevant background material including, where applicable, any PR handouts or newspaper write-ups concerning the host organisation.

Once the completed questionnaire and the rest of the material has been studied, a phone call to the secretary should elicit a great deal of useful and perhaps usable information. For instance, the fact that the chairman of a company whose employees you are to address is a keen sailor could provide useful background material for your speech, while something apparently insignificant – like the information that the doorman is a well loved 'character' who prefaces every statement with: 'Ah well, we'll have to see about that' – could lead to your immediate acceptance by the audience and turn the hall into a comfort zone.

The exact address with details on how to get there is crucial information and 'Just ask for the Trades Hall' is not good enough. Your taxi driver could turn out to be the only person in town who doesn't know there are two halls or that the hall in question is five miles from the station.

You must know exactly what you are being asked to talk about and for how long. 'Perhaps you could talk about the

Civil War for – oh, about the usual half an hour to an hour or so. . .' Perhaps you could, but in public speaking terms half an hour is a marathon and an hour represents 10,800 words – which even at G.B. Shaw's generous estimate of a professional writer's output is about five days' work. It's also a long time to keep people's interest – especially if you are talking about the wrong civil war – and ten to twenty minutes is usually a more sensible length.

Who's going to be there, how many, and what sort of people are they? It's useful to know the average age and perhaps also the racial or religious mix because, even though winners do their damnedest not to give offence, there are some people who are hypersensitive.

THE EARLY WINNER DOESN'T GET THE BIRD

Even when you've done all your homework, it is as well to try to arrive at the venue early to meet the official host and look the place over. If your lateness is genuinely unavoid-able, have a couple of jokes about traffic jams, etc., ready. At this stage, apart from checking that the information to hand is still correct, winners want to know where they will be standing and whether everyone can see them. Does the public address system work properly or does it, when tested, scream like a demented burglar alarm?

Arriving early also gives you a bit of notice if the secretary greets you with an announcement like, 'Joan Collins couldn't make it, so we're putting you in to bat first if that's okay.'

INTRODUCTIONS

Talking of celebrities in his excellent *Complete Speaker's Guide* – which incidentally contains hundreds of anecdotes, jokes and one-liners – comedian Bob Monkhouse stresses that, no matter how well known you may be, you must have someone to introduce you and the person who introduces you must know exactly who you are, even if you have to write it down for them. Winners can make capital out of being wrongly introduced if it does happen, but it usually pays to make sure people get your name right in the first place.

SHOW TIME

So, there you are, facing an indulgent audience, after a glowing and accurate introduction, knowing that you have done everything possible in the way of research to make your speech a winner.

Being aware that electronic sound systems invariably make one drink sound like three, you will have had only one drink, if any, at the reception and one or at the most two glasses of wine with the meal, and realising that speakers are not invisible before they begin speaking, you will not have undermined the impression you intend to make by picking, scratching, guzzling or playing footsie under the table.

In short, you are in pretty good shape and all you need do now is to play your winning cards.

There is a school of thought which considers it best for speakers to have the full text of their speech in front of them when they stand up to speak, and if you are giving a talk crammed with facts and figures to a learned body this could well be the case.

However, most people, with the exception of talented actors and experienced newsreaders, find it difficult to 'get words off the page' as it's called in the trade. This is partly because most of us write very differently from the way we speak and partly because talking with one's eyes fixed on a sheaf of papers is off-putting for the audience. TV newsreaders now get over this by using an Autocue which scrolls down the full text as they read, but they still have a script on the desk as well and alternate between script and screen in order to avoid looking like mad hypnotists.

If the sort of speech you have to give makes a full script essential, it's a winning move to memorise at least some of it and to rehearse, with the help of a recorder and if possible a 'tame' audience. In this way it is possible to avoid things like the script-reader's monotone, the great piece of writing that turns out to be a tongue-twister and the 'how do you people out there like the crown of my head?' look. We much prefer the winner's card trick.

THE CARD TRICK

The card trick alone could make you a winning public speaker, as well as helping you to win with words in meetings, at the negotiating table and even as a tyro salesman.

All you need are a dozen or so file cards and a couple of thick felt pens, one black and one red. Mark the first card at the top with a large '1' in a circle and put an easily remembered one-word 'catchline' in fairly small black letters in the right-hand corner. This prevents you from giving a speech intended for the Licensed Victuallers to the Temperance League.

Then print in block capitals, large enough for you to read at arm's length or from a table top where you are speaking, the place and the name of the group you are addressing because, as President Reagan discovered to his cost, getting either of these points wrong is not a winning move.

Leave a decent space and then print, again in block capitals, the name of the person who is introducing you, together with the names and titles if any of those VIPs whose presence you can check with the secretary. Be generous with cards – but don't forget to number and 'catchline' each one.

Leave one card blank except for its number and catchline, just in case something funny really does happen to you on the way to the hall. Then move into your speech proper, with a memory-jogging note for each point you want to make and names and figures written out in full. Number or letter each card and make sure that there is enough detail about jokes and their punch-lines – especially the punch-lines – to enable you to remember them.

WINNING IS ON THE CARDS

One advantage of the card system over the complete script is that you don't get up to speak clutching or riffling through a huge sheaf of papers, implying that you intend to talk for hours.

More importantly, using cards gives your speech a feeling of spontaneity impossible to achieve by any other method, except perhaps by learning the whole thing by heart and rehearsing it for days, which could easily backfire should you lose the thread of your argument or have an attack of nerves.

Winning is on the cards

Using your flexible friends means you should never suffer from nerves again, especially once you have worked out how much wordage, on average, you can get from a short note. Flexibility really is the appropriate word because you can increase or decrease the wordage from each note according to the feedback you sense from the audience, dropping a less important item if you feel you may be overrunning.

PRACTICAL WINNING

Prepare a set of cards for a speech you might be required to give and then practise it, using a cassette recorder. In the end you may find that you have only to glance at each card fairly briefly in the course of the speech. You may even find that merely having them in your pocket or on the table gives you all the confidence you need.

STAND AND DELIVER

Most people are not good listeners and some experts maintain that audiences on average retain only 15 per cent of any speech they hear.

However, if you were to threaten to have them shot if they failed to answer questions when you finished speaking or offered them £100 for every question they were able to answer correctly, there is little doubt that the retention rate would improve dramatically, which means that motivation is an important factor and that retention can be increased if speakers identify correctly the audience's wants and fears.

Retention can also be improved by the use of vivid language and strong visual imagery or even by simple strategies like informing your audience that the normal retention rate is only 15 per cent; but even so, retention will never be total and in most cases what audiences take away after a speech is a garbled version of the content – including, with luck, a couple of the more important passages – combined with a crystal clear and virtually unforgettable impression of the speaker and the way in which the speech was delivered.

This makes delivery a vital element of any public speech and professional teachers of presentation techniques like actress Avril Carson identify several factors which help to make the spoken word believable and memorable. These include a resonant tone, which is seen as dependable and energetic, a conversational style which gives an impression of sophistication and confidence, and a well paced and varied delivery.

Rate of speech can vary a great deal – standard TV newsreading speed is 3 words a second or 180 a minute – but above 200 or below 110 most speakers lose credibility, while research indicates an audience preference for moderate to fast speakers.

Speakers lose credibility if they are over-formal, repetitive, or if they speak in monotonous, high-pitched, boring or squeaky voices, but many of these handicaps will be automatically overcome if the speaker has a winner's confidence based on research and rehearsal, together with a winner's stance.

A winning stance is one which makes the speaker feel comfortable without sending him or his audience to sleep and confidence will go a long way towards making an open and alert stance automatic. Winners don't hide behind their arms or their script and they make use of movement and gestures without dancing about or flailing. Everything about them proclaims that they have a story to tell and that they know people are going to want to hear it.

Eye contact, with its implications of directness and honesty, is important and the standard advice to public speakers used to be that they should pick out one member of the audience and speak directly to him or her throughout the speech. This undoubtedly gives a hint of intimacy – if not complicity – but it does mean that after a short time the individual concerned will be convinced that you have somehow divined that his fly is undone or that her bra-strap is showing. At the same time the rest of the audience will be feeling vaguely resentful about being neglected. It's much more of a winning move to pick out a dozen friendly faces in different parts of the audience and speak as though you were talking directly to them from time to time, while giving the rest of the hall the occasional benign sweep.

Winners should be courteous to hecklers, if any – at least they were listening – and since hecklers are not usually the type of people who win with words you can always blast them if need be.

Winners are even more courteous to people who ask questions after the speech, especially as this gives them a chance to demonstrate their confidence and their mastery of the subject under discussion. Not only that, but questioners almost certainly *were* listening and if treated with respect bordering on flattery, even when using such classic delaying tactics as, 'I'm glad you asked that . . .', will usually respond by making you more of a winner than you were to begin with.

. . . AND FINALLY

And finally, get it right, keep it short, keep it crisp and keep it simple; remember that it's not as easy to take in a lot of complicated information in oral as in printed form.

Stroke both the audience, their organisation and its officers, where appropriate, bearing in mind that in a speech you can win with the sort of unabashed flattery that would earn you an unwelcome reputation for sycophancy in ordinary conversation.

And even more finally – having made sure in advance

whether there are people in the audience who have to catch buses or trains – *don't overrun*, and do allow time for questions and a few words from your hosts. This not only demonstrates winning good manners but could prevent you from being embarrassed by an unseemly stampede in the middle of your peroration.

Winning Words

The Winners in life think constantly in terms of I can, I will and I am. Losers, on the other hand, concentrate their waking thoughts on what they should have done or what they can't do.

The way I see it, if you want the rainbow, you gotta put up with the rain.
  Dolly Parton (actress and singer)

You can't wait for extraordinary opportunities, you have to seize common occasions and make them great.
  Anita Roddick (chairman, The Body Shop)

Occasional failure is the price of improvement.

4

CODES AND ROLE PLAYING IN THE WORKPLACE

Speaking in public may have its problems but, as we've seen, it does offer winners with words a splendid opportunity, as it is virtually a solo performance and all that need concern us is getting our message across.

Admittedly, communication problems exist in the speaker–audience situation, but to a great extent these can be overcome by the use of appropriate language, effective delivery and vivid imagery, based on an appreciation of the audience's socio-linguistic background.

By contrast, communication involving exchanges between two or more participants is a complicated affair, mainly because, for a variety of reasons (not all of them malicious), people rarely say what they really mean, which makes it essential for winners with words to be not only good speakers but excellent interpreters and decoders.

Some of the reasons for the wide-ranging discrepancies between what people say and what they mean are more obvious than others, but the winner with words must learn to recognise them all and know how to deal with them.

WHAT DO THEY MEAN?

People who deliberately set out to mislead are often easier to cope with than those who do not realise that, for one reason or another, their words are not conveying the meaning they intend. Winners should be on their guard against both intentional and unintentional misleading language, including:

1 Deliberate lies

Phrases like 'I'm going to be honest with you' can betray the deliberate liar, as can the classic body-language telltales of sweaty palms, shifty eyes and tensed fingers. Liars who are insecure may also try to hide as much of their body as possible.

2 Negotiating ploys

Here the usual intention is to gain an advantage rather than to deceive in the long term, but the line is blurred and winners should get in as much practice as possible in detecting verbal ruses, like sudden shifts of emphasis or the use of language specifically intended to disguise the speaker's real meaning. Political meetings, including the televised sessions of Parliament, are ideal training grounds for winners who wish to become first-class ploy detectors.

3 Poor communicators

These are among the most difficult to deal with and include those people who do not say exactly what they mean because they are unable to do so. Foreigners, for example, whose command of English is not as great as they imagine, and English speakers whose vocabulary is faulty, often say things which differ from the meaning they intend to convey. Sometimes they may even say the precise opposite of what they mean and, of course, the better they appear to speak the language, the easier it is to become confused by their relatively infrequent blunders. Because the people in question are honest, their mistakes are sometimes difficult to detect and always difficult to deal with. Winners who suspect that they are faced with someone who is unable to make their meaning clear should ask politely for clarification and insist on rephrasing the exchange, several times if necessary, until they are certain that both parties understand exactly what is meant.

4 Socio-linguistic differences

Among English speakers, 'He speaks my language' is a compliment, but sometimes people who speak English do not appear to speak our language, perhaps because of regional differences or more likely because a different background causes them to give the words they use a different meaning or, at the very least, a different emphasis from our own. Calling someone 'middle class', for example, may well mean one thing when used by a duke and quite another when used by a dustman.

This means that, while English speakers are better off than some primitive tribes – whose members must learn to use what are virtually different languages, depending on the rank, relationship and birthplace of the person they are talking to – winners can benefit a great deal from becoming linguistic chameleons.

5 Codes, slang, jargon and secret languages

We shall be dealing with these later, but it is worth remarking that the use of both codes and slang may be either deliberate or involuntary. Winners will find that their interest in words and language will help them to understand all these specialised forms of communication and gain the acceptance of those who use them.

HELP!

At first glance, the fact that people so often fail to say exactly what they mean looks as though it would make communication impossibly complicated, but we know that people *do* communicate: they chat, converse, speak in public, hold seminars and meetings, make jokes, sell and negotiate. The explanation lies in the word 'exactly', because most of the time honest people say approximately what they mean and are approximately understood. Winners seek to improve on this situation by using words more precisely and by interpreting other people's words more accurately.

EVERYBODY WANTS SOMETHING

Because people so seldom say exactly what they mean, winners – if they are to monitor their own use of words and to interpret and decode statements made by others – need a basic rule which can be used as a guideline in all communication situations. Fortunately, we have already made such an assumption – one which on examination appears to have the universal application of, say, a law of physics, namely, that everyone who attempts to communicate wants something.

Nor is there anything intrinsically wrong in wanting; in fact, it was almost certainly wanting things which led to our ability to speak in the first place. It is really 'wanting' – love being essentially one form of desire – that 'makes the world go round'. While it is all too possible to want the wrong things, winners, as optimists, have to believe that on balance most people want things that are good, useful or, at the very least, harmless.

WHAT DO I WANT? WHAT DO WE WANT? WHAT DO THEY WANT?

If the assumption that everyone who communicates wants something holds good, winners can use it as a yardstick for *all* communication situations, always providing they bear in mind that 'wanting' itself is neither good nor bad.

Everyone who opens their mouth to communicate wants something

We suggest that winners should acquire the habit of asking 'Who wants what?', without any cynical overtones, in every communication situation until it becomes virtually automatic. To this end, we shall be pointing out some obvious uses of this particular yardstick as we go along, but winners will use it even more often.

PRACTICAL WINNING

Before you begin to make use of the assumption that *everyone who uses words to communicate wants something*, you may well wish to test it. Try to think of circumstances in which someone might speak – or communicate in any other way – *without* wanting something.

Don't worry if you can't think of any, or if the ones you do think of – such as altruists, who turn out to want things for other people or perhaps even a reputation for altruism – don't stand up to examination. The more often the assumption proves to be true, the closer it comes to being a rule – or even a law – which makes trying to disprove it a useful exercise in winning with words.

A WINNING RULE

The Everyone Wants Something rule is a very useful tool for winning with words, especially in the workplace, where the way in which we handle words can be of supreme importance. Most of us spend half our waking lives at work, which makes winning at work essential, and as winners our aim should be to become part of a winning group, which is part of a winning department, which in turn is part of a winning organisation.

Of course, almost everything we have already discussed about winning with words has its relevance in the workplace and this, together with our increased interest in words and language, will increase our confidence and make us more interesting people for our colleagues to be with. At the same time, any public speaking we are able to do, on whatever scale, will help us to build on that confidence and in turn enable us to use words in a way that will make us career winners, without making others feel like losers.

WORKING WINS BEGIN WITH THE FAMILY

In our previous book *More Ways to Win*, we've already looked at ways in which we can build our immediate family into a winning team and this ability to win with words in the family can provide a great deal of insight into how we should go about winning in the workplace.

Like our first contact with members of the family, our first encounter with colleagues at the start of the working day should be cheerful without being irritatingly so and any complaints should be wryly humorous ones rather than downright whinges.

Even most of those members of the Jobsworth clan who so frequently find employment as security guards or doormen will eventually respond to a winner's 'Good morning.' Perhaps, after all, they have acquired Jobsworth status as a result of seeing so many miserable faces every day and, as every winner knows, a reformed Jobsworth can be a useful ally.

THE 'FAMILY' GROUP IN THE WORKPLACE

Meanwhile, no matter what position we currently hold, or how high we eventually rise, the people in our immediate working group are of the utmost importance in our ability to win at work. Our workmates on the shop floor, our colleagues in the office, our assistants and secretaries are the people with whom we come into contact every working day. They are our intimate workplace 'family' and although, over a period of time, winners may change or extend their working families, these are the people on whom winners depend for information, support, encouragement, human warmth and protection. If we are to win at work, they must be winners too and the ways in which we can use words to help us achieve this are very similar to those we indentified when discussing how to win with our real families.

GOOD MORNING WINNERS

No need to be sick-makingly effusive, but a cheerful 'Good morning, Jane, Tom (or whoever)', followed if possible by a brief chat, is the best way to greet our working family.

Some employers like to see a 'heads down' start as the clock reaches the hour and, if you can't educate them, it's worth going in a minute or two early for those short exchanges that can make your working family into a winning team, especially in cases where waiting till an official break would be toc late. For instance, a winning group leader might discover something about an individual family member which could be as seemingly trivial as a bad cold or as catastrophic as a bereavement or the break-up of a long-term relationship, but which could in either case seriously affect the team member's work within the group. In such cases, a few winning words could make a friend and supporter for the rest of the working relationship, while the wrong words, or none at all, could make an implacable enemy.

Again, from the viewpoint of enlightened self-interest, a minute or so of chat can provide a useful opportunity for gathering low-grade intelligence, although winners may prefer to think of it as keeping a finger on the pulse of their organisation.

WINNING WITH THE WORKPLACE FAMILY

Whatever his or her position within the family group, the winner's attitude must be one of mutual respect, which means that courtesy counts for a great deal and that winning language must start from first principles with the magic words 'please' and 'thank you'. This may seem simplistic, but we have only to think back to the resentment we felt when someone asked us brusquely, perhaps even rudely, to fetch a file or for that matter to write a company report. Good manners are effective in the workplace and the tone in which winners use words is as important as the words themselves.

Your subordinates may well be paid to do what you are asking them to do, but they will do it better if the way you ask them makes them feel like winners. In addition, good manners in the workplace, as elsewhere, are bankable and enable winners to ask the occasional favour.

WINNING STROKES

'Stroking' in the workplace, especially in the intimate family group, is vital and in many ways it is easier to stroke downwards than upwards. Group leaders can, for instance, use stroking words to compliment team members on their work, or even on their appearance, but it's often difficult to do this in reverse without seeming sycophantic. However, bosses enjoy being complimented as much as anyone, so it is actually quite in order for a junior to compliment a senior on a specific achievement and perhaps once in a while on a new hairstyle or item of clothing.

Like good manners, compliments are bankable, so a winning senior, for instance, who has frequently praised his juniors in this way, can usually criticise them, if need be, without causing any resentment. On such occasions winners will choose their words carefully, having arranged wherever possible to deal with the matter on a one-to-one basis. This helps the reprimanded party not to feel a loser and prevents what should be a discussion, or at most an admonition, developing into an unseemly wrangle.

PRACTICAL WINNING

As the leader or – to use the new winning word – the 'coach' of a small workplace group, you might have occasion to reprimand a team member for persistent bad time-keeping. Use a cassette recorder to note how you might go about this, paying special attention to the words you use and the tone in which you say them.

What did you want? What did your subordinate want? Did you emerge a winner? Would your subordinate have left your office feeling a loser?

If you are not happy with the recording when you play it back, the chances are that you did not decide in advance what you wanted by applying the Everyone Wants Something rule.

IT DEPENDS WHAT YOU MEAN BY WINNING

Professor Joad, a member of the panel on an early broadcast show called 'The Brains Trust', became famous for prefacing his answer to every question with 'Well, it all depends what you mean by . . .', thus winning with words twice – once by gaining thinking time in which to formulate his answers and secondly by finding a phrase which became his nationally known trademark.

As winners with words, it is important for us to define our terms and aims with precision and to decide in any given circumstances what it is that we want and what outcome will constitute a win.

In the case of a persistent latecomer, for instance, what the winner wants is to ensure that the offender arrives at work on time in future, to accomplish this without making the offender feel a loser and even, if possible, to send him out feeling an enthusiastic member of a winning team. What winners do not want is to demonstrate their power, to get rid of their frustrations, or to express anger in words so forcible and ill-chosen as to frighten the culprit, especially as frightened people often withdraw into themselves and make little or no contribution to the group's activities until they recover.

Of course, any of these inappropriate 'wants' might result in a grovelling apology from the offender, which might feel like a win in the short term, but would really be unsatisfactory because of the disproportionate resentment felt by that team member.

The first aim of the winner in a case of this sort should be to save himself work – and possible embarrassment – by finding out as quickly as possible if the offender has any valid excuse for being persistently late. A winning boss should really have found out in the course of – or as a result of – the pre-work informal chat sessions if there was anything seriously amiss, but now has another chance to do so. At this stage, if the culprit reveals a genuine reason for lateness, like serious illness or a death in the family, the interview could end with an offer of help – say, a few hours off or the use of the office phone – or at least some sympathetic words. However, if this is not the case, the winner, knowing that everybody wants something, should ask himself what the tardy subordinate really wants, which could be something as simple as having their desk moved to a less noisy position. At the end of the interview the winning boss might say, 'Well, I'm glad there was no serious problem and I know that you won't let us down in future, so we'll leave it there for the moment, shall we?'

Note that the boss has used a form of code to make his position just as clear as he would have done with a losing version like 'You have no excuse for your persistent lateness, so you'd better not be late again. I've got my eye on you and if you don't shape up, I'm going to come down on you like a ton of bricks!' He also stands a much better chance of a win-win outcome.

ALL THE WORLD'S A STAGE – AND WINNERS ACT COOL

Winners with words keep their temper, whether in one-on-one situations or addressing groups, mainly because they know that losing it will impair their judgement and reduce their winner's edge. However, winners don't necessarily qualify for haloes and there seems no reason why they should lose out on useful ways to win with words, like a show of temper.

This brings us to an aspect of winning with words so important that, had it not been said before, and better, we should have been tempted to put it in capital letters, namely, that the world is a stage and that all of us are actors. This is yet another complicating factor in almost all communication situations, but one which we can simplify by applying the Everyone Wants Something rule, usually by asking 'What do they want to achieve by playing such and such a role?'

WINNERS AND ROLE-PLAYING

We are, in fact, all of us role players and – again to paraphrase Shakespeare – some of us choose our roles and others have their roles thrust upon them. Either way, many of us adopt one role for life and become archetypal old maids, good old boys, martyrs, eccentrics, hearties, fluffy blondes and so on, for ever.

Sadly, some of the roles people adopt, or more often have thrust upon them, are the roles of typical losers: the perpetual subordinate, the yes man, the clown, the punch bag and even the victim. Winners with words can help people like this to shed the worst aspects of their losing roles, but it is not easy as fundamental changes are needed. First, however, if they themselves are to avoid being confined in the straitjacket of a single character part, winners must identify their own major role and learn to shade it into any number of different characters, without detracting from their main personality. Winners with words will have the chameleon ability to shade the character they present to the world by making slight changes in their vocabulary, accent and tone.

Like some actors who are said to 'play themselves', winners can play themselves as heroes, lovers, salesmen, negotiators and so on, as circumstances suggest. Of course we're not implying that winners should be dishonest and counterfeit emotions they don't feel, but merely suggest that – especially in the workplace – they should use their ability to win with words to express their feelings trenchantly and precisely without being carried away by them.

Using the techniques of method acting, by convincing themselves first, winners can project for example the image of a truly angry person. However, as they are role-playing, they will be able to monitor their own performance to make certain they don't turn other people into resentful losers.

THE WINNER'S CRITIC

In order to carry out this sort of role-playing, winners must listen to themselves talking and heed the voice of the 'critic' at the back of their brain – or, to be physiologically accurate, in one hemisphere of it.

This is the 'voice of reason' which constantly monitors and criticises the winner's choice of words, their tone and their emotional content and while most of the time this process is almost automatic, it can be useful to make a conscious effort to listen to oneself every so often when, for example, negotiating or selling.

WINNING WITH CODES

If listening to oneself is important, listening to other people is even more so and, in addition to listening, winners must learn to interpret codes. This is difficult, because half the time most of us use codes of some sort without being aware of it.

With this in mind, it's worthwhile studying the use of codes in some of the communication situations we've already looked at. For instance, most couples and families use a complicated interlocking series of codes which act as intimacy reinforcers within the group and allow for graded access to their linguistic comfort zone for favoured outsiders. Couples within the group will have love codes and many families will have codes of euphemisms for what they consider to be taboo words and topics. Such codes are often associated with 'in' jokes – another comfort zone reinforcer.

These family codes have their counterparts elsewhere, especially in the workplace, where we encounter them most obviously within the intimate 'family' group, being used for precisely the same reasons as in the home: to reinforce the comfort zone of the group and as a security precaution, permitting graded admission to the comfort zone. In addition to group codes, individuals use codes sometimes unwittingly in one-to-one situations. Winners with words know they are succeeding when they are admitted totally or partially into a code-using group who might tell them, 'You know what we mean when we call Friday quitting time "the night of the long envelopes",' or when he or she identifies a girl's 'I'm not really at my best today' as code for 'I have my period and feel like hell'. Code breaking, as in this instance, can help winners to make thoughtful winning decisions.

Other codes which may be encountered outside the home are secret languages (often used by minority groups such as gypsies), slang and jargon. All codes of this sort are combinations of intimacy reinforcers, security measures, peer group recognition signals and means of maintaining exclusivity, whilst permitting access to the group to selected outsiders. Demonstrating that one has broken a particular code, as when police use the same slang as criminals, can also be a form of ego booster.

PRACTICAL WINNING

Identify codes within your own family and translate them on the lines of 'I'm not all that keen on going round to Jennifer's again' – translation: 'You know I can't stand Jennifer's husband'; or 'Is there anything you particularly want to watch at eight o'clock?' – translation: 'I'd like to watch the gardening programme, so you're going to have to record the thriller'; 'I'll just take the dog for a walk' – translation: 'I'll just nip down to the pub for an hour'. Similarly, identify codes in use in your own workplace family group and any into which you have been initiated outside your group. If jargon is used in your particular workplace, identify any instances in which it may have been used not to simplify communication but to make life difficult for outsiders.

CODE BREAKING TO WIN

Application of the Everyone Wants Something rule will help us to break codes of all sorts by determining people's self-image and pinpointing what it is that they really want.

Most people's wants are self-orientated, but there is a vital difference between egocentricity and egotism. Winners, if they are to be all-round winners, want a great deal for both themselves and others and realise that in order to produce this desirable win-win situation by conversations, meetings, discussions or negotiations, they must first decide what they really want and what other people really want. Only then can they win with words.

Winning Words

Enthusiasm is not just an outward expression, once you acquire it, it constantly works within you.
Dale Carnegie

He that lives upon hope will die fasting.
Ben Franklin

Reach out for your goal and you will achieve it.
Paul Gascoigne (England international footballer)

Everyone wants to smoke the peace pipe, but no one wants to fetch the tobacco.
Brazilian proverb

5

WINNING AT MEETINGS

Meetings are important communication situations where decisions are made which, in the short or long term, affect the lives of those who attend them and often those of others.

In the workplace, they are gatherings which have a specific and useful function in the running of an organisation and in consequence until recently the meeting, with its echoes of Board Meetings, was seen as the prerogative of higher management. In fact so great was the mystique which came to surround the word that even today some senior executives confess to being slightly apprehensive at the thought of having to attend a 'meeting'. This is a pity as more and more organisations are discovering that meetings are an ideal way to involve and motivate not only managers and executives but the whole of the workforce.

For winners with words, meetings provide splendid opportunities to put over their ideas, to contribute to the functioning of the organisation and to achieve recognition so that, far from being worried by meetings, winners look forward to them.

Those who do feel any lingering apprehension can use techniques we have already come across to dispel any awe-inspiring connotations the word may have – for instance, a check on the definition of the word indicates that a meeting is merely 'an assembly or gathering', which robs it of much of its mystique and at the same time renders it rather bland and uninteresting.

Further investigation, however, reveals a connection with the Anglo-Saxon 'gemot', giving 'meeting' a hint of 'to moot' or to bring up for discussion, together with a suggestion of 'moot' or debatable point, and of 'moot courts' in which lawyers and law students tried hypothetical legal cases. Even more pertinent is the connection with the 'Witangemot' – the gathering of 'wise' senior churchmen and nobles who came together to advise Anglo-Saxon kings.

Looked at in any of these ways there is very little about meetings that should make us feel apprehensive about attending them, and every reason for us to feel flattered at being considered wise enough for our counsel to be of value.

Evidently, the discovery that the reasoning power of any meeting will usually be greater than the sum of the reasoning abilities of the individuals taking part was an early one and, while it's amusing to think of the Anglo-Saxon kings calling their wisest and most experienced men together for the brain-storming sessions which were the precursors of today's Parliament, it does give some idea of the important functions meetings can perform.

Incidentally the vogue word for the phenomenon involving the effect of two or more elements which work together to produce an effect greater than the sum of their individual effects is 'synergy', a word which came originally from the Greek via Latin as syn+ergon, or with+work, which underlines the importance of committees as a way of working together. Meetings are in fact so important it seems a pity to cheapen their function by using the word either to boost someone's ego or as a catch-all excuse for non-availability by announcing that So-and-so is 'in a meeting' when what is meant is that they are simply not around or are too busy to be bothered.

Instead, the usefulness of meetings at all levels of most organisations should be recognised by introducing them as normal practice for the whole of the workforce, which will serve both to demystify them and to add to their inherent value the important functions of training sessions and talent-spotting opportunities.

With this in mind, at junior levels, the 'moot court' aspect of meetings should be emphasised by dealing with hypothetical issues of the sort that participants might later expect to encounter in earnest.

INFORMAL OR FORMAL?

There is of course no need for meetings to be particularly formal. We know one married couple, for instance, who run a successful small business together. They hold a meeting at least once a day, usually over coffee or a drink, to discuss current and future activities and the one thing which makes these get-togethers 'meetings', as opposed to chats or conversations, is that a record is kept of what is said and what decisions are made.

Note-taking, together with the hint of formality it introduces, is normally the distinguishing aspect of a meeting, and in the workplace an informal chat usually becomes a meeting when the senior person present calls the group to order and asks someone to take a note of the proceedings. Incidentally, omitting to do this, because of some vague feeling that everyone in the room is a superior human being and a friend, may make meetings more fun, but it's asking for trouble when somebody says, for example, 'But I didn't agree to order 300,000 widgets.'

WHEN IS A MEETING NOT A MEETING?

The transition from the proto-meeting – an informal chat which is very nearly a meeting – to a formal meeting is an interesting one, and one which varies according to participants and circumstances.

The proto-meetings themselves will vary in nature and can be held in the local pub or in the office, very often with everyone including senior and junior people on first-name terms.

For winners with words, whatever their position in the hierarchy, such occasions provide splendid opportunities. For the winning group leader, for example, they can be the place to make soundings, to hear new and interesting ideas and even, if he has a winner's confidence, to encourage his associates, especially the juniors, to be critical of his policies. For junior winners they provide opportunities for brain-storming and for putting forward ideas and suggestions on topics which, under more formal conditions, might be considered beyond their scope.

The proto-meeting is also an excellent place for winning group leaders to ensure that all the men in their team are helping to make the family group into a comfort zone for any women team members. Of course they will have picked a team of well mannered winners in the first place, but it's up to them to make certain that young women newcomers are not harassed by suggestive remarks and perpetual use of foul language. The trouble is that it is easy for men to develop a group speech style containing both these elements as a group intimacy reinforcer, without realising that what seems like good hearted, all-lads-and-lasses-together banter may well be offensive to many girls and women.

Winning women team members can do a great deal to

ensure that the workplace is a comfort zone for everyone, including the shy and even the prudish. They can use winning words to point out, for instance, that a fellow team member is being upset or to stress that they themselves don't like to be called sweetie or to have everyone assume, unless it is part of her duties, that one of the women rather than a male junior will always make the coffee.

In such cases winning women may well find escalation useful, proceeding from, say, 'I'd prefer it if you didn't call me sweetie, sweetie . . .' via 'I've asked you not to do that,' to 'If you do that again I shall drop a typewriter on your foot.'

In the end, though, it will be the group senior – male or female – who sets the tone for the treatment of women group members by the careful use of winning words, ensuring with a winner's enlightened self-interest a comfortable workplace environment and a better input to the group's tasks than might otherwise have been the case.

Naturally, the group leader will use the formal meeting to reinforce the attitude towards women members already established in proto-meetings and, should the point ever need to be made officially, the meeting proper is the place to do it.

CHANGING GEAR

Sometimes the change from proto-meeting to meeting proper can be made by simply calling the group to order, but it is often a good idea to make a break both in time and venue.

In the formal meeting, as we've seen, notes are taken, and in some organisations first-name terms may no longer seem appropriate. What is important is that winning leaders should make sure that all valid suggestions or criticisms emerging from the proto-meeting, especially those made by juniors, should be acknowledged and presented for more formal discussion at the meeting. Juniors should feel that although their ideas may have been filtered and rephrased they are still recognisably theirs and are being accorded serious consideration. For example the 'That sounds like a good idea, Samantha – what do you think George?' of the proto-meeting becomes at the meeting proper 'Samantha has come up with a plan which may help avoid a recurrence of the recent shortage of widgets. Now what she's suggesting is this . . . I think it will make life easier for all of us, and if we are all agreed – especially George and Jack who know more about widgets than most of us – we'll put Samantha's plan into operation on a trial basis and see how it works out in practice.'

There are one or two potentially winning words here. For one thing, Samantha has been complimented in front of the group and her idea has been acknowledged, which will make her feel a winner with a corresponding increase in her enthusiasm and her willingness to put forward more ideas. Samantha, in other words, will become more of a winning team player in the future. At the same time, since the winning leader has been careful to consult everyone in the group – even though the 'I think . . .' points the way he or she would like things to go – there should be no feelings of resentment towards Samantha and everyone should leave the meeting feeling like a winner.

WHAT – NO HYMN?

The workplace family group which exists at all levels of corporate life is often much like a small comfort zone kingdom with its own language, its own rules and its own 'foreign policy'. All such groups must function efficiently both individually and together with other such groups if the workforce and ultimately the organisation are to win. Winners who head up this sort of workplace family group will probably hold a semi-formal to formal meeting daily, or at least on a regular basis, and in addition to having notes made will prepare an agenda to make sure that nothing is missed out.

This is the time for individual praise and for group praise – and criticism. It is also the time for ironing out any technical or procedural difficulties within the group. It is not really the time for discussing whether ginger biscuits or currant buns should be served with morning coffee, although the importance of such questions could be acknowledged by the immediate formation of a small *ad hoc* committee to canvass and report back, thus avoiding wasting valuable time while side-stepping something which might finish up as the great currant bun row that brought the widget industry to a standstill. Winning teams would probably have decided long ago to have both, anyway.

Even meetings at which the group leader has felt the need to be critical should finish on an upbeat note, enabling the team leader to close the meeting with a few morale-boosting words.

As we mentioned when discussing public speaking, it is often possible to use more emotive language when speaking to a group than when talking to individuals. Mind you, we are not suggesting that all workplace groups should go the full Japanese route with rousing morning performances of the company anthem, but it is acceptable to be a little more gung-ho at meetings than in one-to-one situations.

There's perhaps no need to go the full Japanese route

EVERYONE WHO ATTENDS A MEETING WANTS SOMETHING

Looking at the derivation of the word 'meeting' has provided some insights into the function of this particular sort of gathering and we can now apply the Everyone Wants Something rule to determine how winning with words can help us to win at meetings.

Of course every meeting is different, but in general terms, at meetings of the workplace family group, for example, the leader will want to build the morale of the team members, to increase their effectiveness and to make them more productive, while at the same time helping them to become individual winners.

From a personal point of view, leaders will want to achieve recognition from their hierarchical superiors as the leader of a winning team and to secure from team members admiration, liking and respect, adding up to an unofficial endorsement of their position as leader of the group. This acknowledgement by the team that the leader, whatever their title, is in fact the boss, the chief, the governor, the 'Dragon Lady' or the 'Old Man', is an important way in which to win with words. Imposing titles and a big office may be useful trappings but in these days, when the workplace leader is more of a coach than a policeman, it is the genuine effect that words can evoke which will help the leader to become a winner.

This multiple motivation of 'help self–help group– help organisation' type, triggered by enlightened self-interest, is echoed by the members of the group who also wish to win – in this case by making an acknowledged contribution to the meeting.

THE WIN–WIN MEETING

There should be no real conflict of interests here although there may well be personality clashes and differences of opinion on how to achieve team aims.

Not all team members will be genuine team players and there will sometimes be characters like the Machiavelli of the workplace who would rather plot than plan, but whose machinations can be defeated by asking 'What exactly does Machiavelli want?'

Winners with words know how to recognise the Machiavellis and the Jobsworths, how to render them harmless and convert them to team players or how to get rid of them. They are experts at unruffling ruffled feathers, even those of team members who know they could do the leader's job better than the leader can but who can usually be persuaded to play the role of 'brilliant, loyal – if superior – counsellor'.

Winners, whatever their position in the group, will first determine what it is that they themselves want from the meeting and what they wish the meeting to achieve. They can then assess – or, if they already know, take into account – the roles various participants in the meeting have been assigned or have assigned themselves, and concentrate all their energies on getting everyone to work together for a win–win outcome.

PRACTICAL WINNING

Try as far as possible to achieve total recall of the last meeting you attended and to establish the roles being played by those taking part. Examine the various 'virtuosi' as opposed to team player performances and ask yourself how the meeting could have been improved, especially by applying the Everyone Wants Something rule and by aiming for a win–win outcome.

If you were the group leader, ask yourself how a better understanding of other people's wants could have helped make it a more successful and productive meeting.

SYNERGY AND THE WELL DESIGNED CAMEL

There was once a cynical view of the usefulness of meetings which was encapsulated in the saying that 'a camel is a horse designed by a committee'. The implication was that the diversity of opinions and background knowledge inherent in any decision-making group could only produce a hotch-potch result as unlovely as the camel.

Of course the camel, while not noted for pulchritude, is superbly adapted to the conditions in which it lives and would be a tribute to the synergism of any committee which had designed it. Nevertheless, the saying does make the point that there can be a downside to meetings which, unless well planned and well run, can become too numerous, too wordy and too time-consuming.

However, largely because of the synergetic element, meetings perform a vital function in today's business and corporate life, so much so that the more important an individual's function the greater is the proportion of their time they will normally spend in meetings.

This is because the phenomenon of synergy, which ensures that the effects generated by a meeting will normally be greater than the sum of the individual effects, also ensures that the effects of several meetings working together through the medium of a super meeting or meetings will be greater than the sum of the effects of individual meetings.

All this really means, of course, is that winners who decide that what they really want is to get as close to the top of any given organisation as is compatible with their remaining a winner must be able to win with words – at meetings.

Winning Words

Meetings are like cocktail parties. You don't want to go, but you're cross not to be asked.
Jilly Cooper (author)

If you don't blow your own trumpet, nobody will blow it for you . . . But make sure you play the right tune!
Lord Forte (chairman, Trusthouse Forte)

The most favourable opportunity always occurs at the most inopportune moment.

6

WINNING AT SEMINARS

Most winners with words find meetings enjoyable as well as useful, and as long as a communication situation can still be recognised as a get-together of the home team, with its 'conversational' aspect intact, it remains a meeting.

It is when communication situations shift into a teaching mode that they become 'lectures' or 'seminars', both of which sound impressive, even daunting, probably because of their associations with universities. However, even at university the distinction is made between formal lectures and the less formal seminars in which students are encouraged to participate, and there is no reason why seminars should not be enjoyable. In fact, away from the university environment, the entertainment character of seminars is often deliberately emphasised.

Lectures are merely a particular form of public speaking and the word itself, with its derivation from the Latin 'legere', to read, indicates its formal character as a speech that is more often than not read from a prepared text.

Seminars, on the other hand, are gatherings at which an expert or experts address a group of delegates, each talk being followed by questions from the floor, group discussions or both. It's this participation aspect which makes them such ideal occasions on which to win with words, and adds a social element which, as many businesses have been quick to appreciate, makes seminars an extremely effective method of getting their message across.

Of course the aim of winners, whether giving or attending seminars, should be to ensure that all parties finish up by winning, and this is especially the case now that seminars – once the prerogative of executive grades – are common at all levels of most medium-sized and large organisations. This increasing appreciation of the value of seminars is splendid but, as with 'meetings', there is a danger of debasing our verbal currency by over-using the word 'seminar' when something like 'discussion group' is more appropriate.

SOWING THE SEEDS IN SEMINARS

As we've seen, checking the meaning and derivation of words is a good way to demystify them and at the same time to discover shades of meaning which might otherwise be overlooked. In this respect the derivation of 'seminar' is particularly apposite, as it comes, via German, from the Latin 'seminarium' or 'nursery garden', and is closely related to both seeds and semen – a winner will take care to select the right site, seeds and conditions, as well as tending the plants once they have taken root.

JUST ANOTHER FEW WORDS

One of the good things about winning with words is that the skills we acquire in one sector can almost always be applied in another, so that once we have begun to win with words we never again have to start from scratch.

This means that winners who have been broadening their reading range, polishing up their conversational skills, taking part in meetings and talking in public – if only at family gatherings – can feel quite confident if they are asked to give a seminar. They know that they will be using their public-speaking skills to sow seeds of information which will germinate in the form of participation from the floor, at which time they will use their conversational ability to direct and control the discussion.

The only new element, in fact, will be the high informational content of most speeches presented at seminars and the mandatory, rather than voluntary, participation of the audience. This means that while, from the speaker's point of view, much of the preparation for seminars is similar to that needed for other forms of public speaking, there is usually a need for even more preliminary work.

PREPARING TO WIN

In the case of seminars the choice of venue is important, as is the timing, but these are largely organisational matters – although winners who are not in overall charge of the whole affair will check that they are not being asked to hold a seminar for potential clients in, say, an old Scout hut.

The venue should reflect the participants' normal working conditions, with standards of comfort perhaps a little higher than they are accustomed to, and many winners who have the chance to pick their own ground now opt for hotels with conference facilities. Many of these now provide a package deal which includes receptions and meals, conference room with public address system, first-class lighting and visual aids like slide projectors, as well as secretarial facilities and adequate communication systems. The latest trend is for stately homes to provide seminar facilities of this type, with office suites, restaurants, bars and drawing rooms furnished in the appropriate grand manner. Naturally this sort of thing is fairly costly but it's difficult not to conclude that a glass or two of champagne in the Great Hall will facilitate the task of winning with words enormously.

Unless they have already used a particular venue – and perhaps even then – winners should check out the facilities in advance. We once suffered agonies of embarrassment, as well as almost killing ourselves trying not to laugh, when a bunch of Savile Row-suited PR consultants gave a 'We-Are-The-Greatest' seminar-type presentation to some newly acquired clients at which everything went wrong, including screaming microphones and upside-down visual aids.

It is difficult to win with words when faced with disasters of this sort, so winners check – and then double check. In fact in the case of seminars, as with almost all communication situations, while the words themselves are of prime importance, presentation is vital if we are to get our message across.

This means that the speaker's delivery should be good, that everyone connected with the organising of the seminar should be smartly and appropriately dressed, and that the venue and even the smallest items like notepads should be of the best quality the budget will stand. What we should aim for, if the seminar is to be memorable, is a touch of the style and panache that marks out the winner.

SPEAKING WITH THE BOOK

Companies which give frequent seminars may well have specially prepared kits including glossy handouts which are sent to participants or are waiting for them on their arrival. Winners will also have sent out an invitation to each participant – perhaps computer-personalised – giving the names of the speaker or speakers, the address and telephone number of the venue, together with a map and possibly a schedule. They may well stress the enjoyable aspects of the seminar by heading their letters with something like 'You are cordially invited to a champagne reception. . .'

Handouts, glossy or not, are essential, especially if masses of statistics are involved, but notes of speeches should be distributed at the end of the seminar rather than before it, giving them a 'hot off the press' immediacy which makes them more effective and obviating the need for either reading along with the speech or note-taking, both of which are annoying for speaker and audience alike.

Whether or not to provide a glossy kit and expensive souvenirs – the derivation from the French for 'remember' indicates their value – is a matter of economics, but a good rule of thumb is that while tasteful elegance is splendid and utilitarian plainness entirely acceptable, any hint of the tawdry is totally self-defeating.

WINNING ICE-BREAKERS

As the managing director of Industrial Motivation Ltd, Nick Thornely spends much of his working life organising and presenting seminars and believes that creating the right climate as people arrive is an essential factor that is often neglected.

There has to be a proper check-in procedure and the people attending the seminar must know precisely what time they are expected and when they should check in and be given their name-tags. Winning organisers, we suggest, could make a feature of greeting the delegates themselves rather than leaving this all-important initial contact to secretaries or receptionists, especially those employed by the venue which, while it fulfils the function of checking which of the people who agreed to take part have actually arrived, is about as personal as booking a train ticket.

The next thing that almost always happens after the check-in is that people wander round looking lost because they don't know anyone, a situation which – while tailor-made for winners with words who are practised in inaugurating conversations – is far from a winning way to organise a seminar. Like the proto-meeting before the formal meeting, and the meal before the speech, an ice-breaking informal get-together of some sort is an essential part of any seminar.

Nick Thornely likes to get his seminars off to a flying start with a champagne breakfast – usually featuring Buck's Fizz so that non-drinkers can choose just orange juice – which gives the participants a sense of occasion and helps to eliminate the classroom atmosphere which can make winning with words difficult.

One technique which works well is to assign a host to each group of delegates as soon as they arrive who also acts as the table host for the breakfast. The hosts are briefed in advance on delegates' names, including first names and positions, so that they can make comprehensive introductions which not only promotes a comfortable atmosphere but also creates sub-groups of eight to ten people within the group, which is extremely useful when smaller units are needed to take part in discussions or prepare questions.

Obviously delegates should be relaxed at the end of the reception or breakfast rather than knee-walking tight and this introductory session, like all other happenings throughout the day, should be carefully timed. Most people are anxious to get on with the seminar, so five minutes is the maximum leeway that should be allowed at each point in the programme.

THE UNSPOKEN CONTRACT

Most people who attend seminars, even though they may have paid to do so, expect that they will hear a great many things that they know already and don't mind this as it is a reassuring confirmation of their own abilities. They will be more than satisfied if, in addition, they can pick up a certain amount of new information, but they will always be put off by poorly presented speeches.

Here again, as in the case of public speaking, there is an unspoken contract between the speaker and the delegates to the effect that the speaker will provide information and entertainment in exchange for courteous attention and intelligent participation. However, as most seminars are held during working hours, the entertainment factor represents a considerable bonus for the participants.

This gives speakers with the ability to win with words a great advantage. They will, for instance, have acquired enough inside information to enable them to begin the proceedings with a joke; where appropriate, they will know how to stroke the host organisation or individual delegates but they will not belittle the delegates and they will not use their superior knowledge of their own subject to talk down to them or to make them feel small.

Winning organisers and speakers resist the temptation to show off and instead turn their seminars into comfort zones, partly because it is easier to speak in a relaxed, pleasant atmosphere, but mainly because they know that even some otherwise tough executives can become unaccountably shy when asked to speak to a group of strangers and these people, more than anyone, need to be made to feel winners.

Speakers who experience difficulty in getting their listeners to participate may find that beginning the day with hosted groups will help, while short sessions will allow delegates to take in information more easily than long ones. Thirty minutes, plus a few minutes for questions, is about right, as it takes a brilliant speaker to fill as much as an hour, even allowing for discussions, and it is better to set a time which leaves the delegates complaining that the session was too short, rather than to have a – literally – yawning gap in which nobody has anything pertinent to say.

WINNING FROM THE BODY OF THE KIRK

From the delegate's point of view, a winning seminar is one which they thoroughly enjoy and which they leave feeling that they have been made privy to at least a little information, perhaps difficult to acquire in any other way, which will be useful to their organisation and possibly helpful to them in their business or their career. In addition to gaining information from the speakers, they may well have made useful contacts among their fellow delegates, and winning organisers should encourage this by preparing lists of delegates containing as much information as possible.

Winning delegates will experience no difficulty in speaking from the floor or in discussion groups and may well make useful contributions which make them feel good and earn them the recognition of their peers. They will usually have made things easier for themselves in this respect by some pre-seminar intelligence-gathering, perhaps in the form of a phone call to a friend who has attended a similar seminar. Knowing that winners don't 'switch-off', they will listen attentively to the speaker or speakers – a courtesy which could enable them to win with a single well observed and well expressed contribution. They will certainly not make themselves objectionable to all concerned by making frivolous or badly thought out comments and interruptions. As the Americans put it, in one of their distinctly winning contributions to the English language, 'nobody loves a smart-ass'.

Like the speakers, who will have made arrangements to follow up the seeds they have sown at the seminar with phone calls and letters, winners will have prepared to go on winning by taking notes, so that they can make a report on the seminar for their own organisation if requested to do so. In this connection, a winning move for delegates is to travel to and from seminars by train which provides a splendid opportunity to review seminar documents and to make a mental or actual note of any particularly winning words. Drive back to your home or office, say the experts, and it's unlikely that you will look at the documents again.

EVERYONE AT SEMINARS WANTS SOMETHING

A winning seminar from the point of view of the organisers, the speakers and the participants, is one in which everyone wins and from which the delegates in particular go away feeling that they would, if necessary, have attended in their own time and paid with their own money.

Winners, whether organisers or delegates, will of course have applied the Everyone Wants Something rule and asked themselves what they hope to gain from the seminar and what the organisers and other delegates want. Occasionally the answers to this sort of question surprise even the experts. For instance, a recent survey aimed at discovering what delegates to seminars wanted from the coffee breaks revealed that nobody was in the least interested in the coffee and that what concerned them most was the availability of telephones and fax machines.

This smacks of workaholism but it does indicate a dedication to winning with words of the highest order. However, we are not quite so sure about the findings of another survey by the Department of Trade and Industry which showed that it is difficult to persuade some senior people to attend seminars if they consider the fees to be too low. Mind you, we feel certain that there will be one or two winners with words who will be happy to organise seminars for this sort of delegate, with fees which will get into the *Guinness Book of Records*, and to provide them with embossed certificates of attendance into the bargain.

Of course, as we've mentioned, there is nothing wrong with giving seminars a cachet of distinction, but overly high fees seems a peculiar way to do it. On the other hand, an attractive and distinctive folder, which delegates will be pleased to add to the permanent contents of their briefcase, can become a useful recognition symbol for seminar 'old boys' and enable the winning with words to continue.

One thing many delegates want is a chance to discuss things with the speaker after he or she has finished talking, so winning speakers should demonstrate their commitment by remaining on hand for at least a few minutes.

Organisers should also be prepared to follow up their contacts with delegates not just immediately after the seminar but on an annual basis, even if it is merely a question of a short hand-out. After all, running a productive nursery garden takes time and patience as well as knowledge, dedication, first-class seeds, healthy plants and fertile soil, but it's an exercise which can be extremely rewarding.

Winning Words

You cannot teach a man anything, you can only help him to find it within himself.
  Galileo

Practice does not make perfect. Perfect practice makes perfect.
  Vince Lombardi

The only way to discover the limits of the possible is to go beyond them into the impossible.

For a company to be successful it must have a top class management team and be able to harness their entre-preneurial drive and energy. I call this 'orchestrating anarchy'.
  Sir Allen Sheppard (chairman & group chief executive, Grand Metropolitan PLC)

7

NEGOTIATING TO WIN

Most of us begin negotiating long before we know the meaning of the word and a baby crying to be fed is engaged in fairly sophisticated negotiations as soon as its demands carry the implicit offer that when they are satisfied it will stop crying. From that moment on, most of us are engaged in some sort of negotiation for the rest of our lives, and the things we learn from our early transactions can be of great value when we begin to negotiate in the workplace and elsewhere.

In fact, one of the great lessons about negotiating, at whatever level, can be learned from the wailing infant and its parents who, at first sight, appear to be in what specialists in the art of negotiation describe as an 'adversarial' situation, whereas, in reality, they are not implacable enemies but two parties, each with their own interests, who are in search of a mutually satisfactory solution to their problems.

In most cases the child and its parents love each other, but there is often a time, before negotiations get underway, when infanticide seems an attractive solution – a situation frequently paralleled in negotiations between adults.

In the child–parent situation, a specific problem is usually resolved by the agreement of the party of the first part to stop screaming in return for food, soothing words and, maybe, a bonus cuddle – an outcome which satisfies both parties.

Negotiations between adults tend to be more formal and protracted but the ideal result remains that of a win–win solution.

The ideal result remains that of a win–win solution

WIN–WIN, NOT WIN–LOSE

Winners will have recognised 'win–win' as one way of expressing the central idea put forward in this book and our earlier books on winning – namely that real winners win by ensuring, as far as possible, that other people become winners as well. The phrase is now used by most specialists in the art of negotiation to describe the ideal outcome of any negotiation and encapsulates the idea of an honourable draw, satisfaction for both parties and quantifiable achievements on both sides – in fact a winner's result.

NEGOTIATIONS ARE A SERIOUS BUSINESS

Of course, it's all very well to say that we spend most of our lives negotiating, and so we do, but in order to discuss the art as it affects the more serious aspects of our business and social lives we have to define it more precisely. Fortunately the derivation of the word can help us once again and here the source of the word makes it easy to distinguish between a negotiation and, say, a discussion, as the word 'negotiation' is derived from the Latin 'negotium' or business, which in turn was derived from 'nec-otium' meaning 'not leisure'.

This earlier source gives us the meaning of the word in the way we shall use it and makes it clear, for example, that, while we can have family negotiations as well as business and political negotiations, they will be formal, non-leisure family occasions conducted in a businesslike way, perhaps around the dining table, as opposed to family discussions held in the sitting room against a background of TV.

Mind you, there is no reason why such family occasions should be acrimonious and treating serious family talks of this sort as businesslike negotiations can often take much of the sting out of disagreements about money or property, especially if we bear in mind that winning negotiators will be aiming for a win–win resolution. Not that anyone would wish to have too many family negotiations of this sort. Life's too short to run ordinary family affairs in this way and one of the advantages of a reasonably happy family is that many quite serious problems can be settled with a few words and a handshake. However, the fact that such formal gatherings do occur means that many of us will have gained some experience of family negotiations, which will be useful when negotiating in the workplace and elsewhere.

FORGET THE PRE-FIGHT GLARES

Winners will have learned from family negotiations that the first pitfall to avoid is the squaring-up, complete with hard stares and muscle-flexing, which announces that a fight is about to begin. It's much better to make sure that everyone is comfortable and that, if possible, they have a drink or a cup of coffee while chatting about neutral subjects before getting down to business – a break which could be marked by actually sitting down round the table.

DON'T INSULT AUNTY

Another easy trap to fall into, when holding family negotiations, is the temptation to insult the opposite faction and to rake up old scores going back anything up to half a century. Cries of 'Everyone knows Aunt Jane can't be trusted – remember how she behaved with that waiter in Marbella?' don't help with negotiations to decide the future of the family holiday home.

This is equally, or perhaps more, important in the workplace where winning with words is as much a question of words to avoid as of words to use, and where phrases like 'you never' and 'you always', delivered in an accusatory tone, can make the resolving of problems difficult, if not impossible.

Often, whether in the home or in the workplace, all that is needed is the use of precise language rather than generalisations. How many times, for instance, does 'you never', as in 'you never help with the washing-up', really mean 'you rarely' – or 'you always', as in 'you are always late with your deliveries', mean 'you are occasionally'?

PRACTICAL WINNING

Make your own list of losing words and phrases which might prejudice negotiations with the family or elsewhere on the lines of the following examples:

'You're completely wrong.'

'You're talking like an idiot.'

'You keep coming up with the same old load of rubbish.'

'That's just childish nonsense.'

Now translate your losing phrases into words more likely to be winners, like:

'I'm not a hundred per cent in agreement with you there.'

'Do you think it would be wise to assume that . . . ?'

'We frequently have difficulty in fully understanding your position.'

'Perhaps if we were to take a more mature view . . .'

Of course you have said much the same thing in both cases, but in the winning version – the greater length of which indicates careful consideration – the choice of 'softer' words means that you won't have forced your opposite to quit the table in high dudgeon – a phrase which originally meant 'waving daggers in the air', which gives a very fair picture of a breakdown in negotiations.

Note that in our examples, and almost certainly in yours, the winning versions contain more polite Norman-French words than blunt Anglo-Saxon ones, and while there is definitely a place in most negotiations for forthright Anglo-Saxon honesty and plain speaking, these should not be used to insult the opposite faction or their arguments.

THE ATTRACTION OF OPPOSITES

'Opposites' may not always attract but they certainly don't invariably repel, which is what makes the word – now used by specialists in the art of negotiation to describe the other faction or factions in a negotiation – such a winner.

Merely by using this word, the man or woman on the other side of the table becomes our 'opposite' rather than our 'opposition' and, at a stroke, the adversarial image of negotiations is lessened while, at the same time, the possibility of reaching a win–win solution is vastly increased.

However, the fact that we are no longer dealing with an 'enemy' doesn't mean that we no longer want the best possible outcome for ourselves, and winners with words will always do some thorough pre-negotiation homework.

WINNERS NEGOTIATE WITH PEOPLE

Winners with words do not negotiate with the Wheeltappers and Shunters' Association as such, but with human beings like Mr Jones, Mr Smith and Mrs Parker, who are experienced officers of the WSA. They recognise that Jones, Smith and Parker – whom they already think of as Martin Jones, Fred Smith and Liz Parker – are individuals and, unless they have met them before, they will already have collected background information on each of them and possibly opened a file, showing their full names, family status, family and educational background, career details, hobbies, likes and dislikes and even prejudices.

This may sound a bit cloak and dagger but in fact most of the information – like 'prefers tea to coffee' or 'farming background' – can usually be obtained from the person's secretary or from published reports and journals.

The important thing is not to go into negotiations without being aware of any way in which you might gain or lose an advantage by choosing the right or wrong words. If you can find words that make your opposites feel good, you are winning – if you distress them, you lose.

TIME FOR A POW-WOW

After finding out about one's opposites, it's time for a 'caucus' or a private get-together of your negotiating team.

The word, which has now been adopted by professional negotiators, is used by American politicians to describe a closed meeting of the delegates of one party, but 'caucus' was originally derived from an Algonquian word meaning 'advisor'. Its main use is to describe the perfectly legitimate negotiating tactic of taking time out from negotiations to go into a private huddle, either whispered or outside the negotiating chamber.

A pre-negotiation caucus – even a last-minute one – is essential if winners are to be able to discuss their opposites and make a note of potential winning or losing words. It also helps to establish if any members of the home team have opposites with similar interests or specialities to their own and are therefore not merely opposites but potential 'opposite numbers'. This can be very useful in establishing rapport in the course of negotiations, and the fact that the phrase was the origin of the army word 'oppo' or mate indicates that finding one or more opposite numbers may help move the negotiations along and keep them on a friendly basis.

PRACTICAL WINNING

The file on Fred Smith could show that in spite of an uncompromising regional accent and a hail-fellow-well-met manner, Fred has a first-class Oxbridge degree in Economics and is a Methodist lay preacher. Winning recommendations might include: avoid talking about 'student layabouts' or hinting that it might be an idea to get a move on in order to finish 'before the pubs shut'. Prepare imaginary short files on Martin Jones and Liz Parker, together with appropriate recommendations for your team.

DECIDE WHAT YOU ARE NEGOTIATING FOR

As everybody who opens their mouths to speak wants something, it follows that everyone who comes to the negotiating table must want something – even it is only to demonstrate their willingness to attend, to make a show of intransigence or to maintain the status quo.

Getting people to the negotiating table is often half the battle and, having achieved this, winners must then decide at the pre-negotiation caucus exactly what it is they want – and what they would settle for – together with what they think their opposites want and what they would settle for. Deciding on one and making the best possible estimate of the other is not always easy, but it is at this stage – and not during the negotiations – that any differences of opinion about aims and strategy between members of the home team should be settled.

A basic question which should be resolved at this stage – or at least very early – is the extent of the opposites' mandate. There is little worse, when negotiating at any level, than the realisation that your opposites do not have the authority to make the concessions you have decided to press for, in addition to which, making certain of their negotiating powers from the start will prevent unscrupulous opposites announcing – when all the cards seem to be on the table – that they are not empowered to grant the very point which has been negotiated. Another thing to settle at the pre-negotiation caucus is what, if any, tactics might be useful and the allocation of roles such as 'good cop–bad cop' to the individuals who will play them.

However, it is essential to remember at this stage that a plan is only a plan, and that while strategic aims should be fixed – within fairly wide parameters – winners with words use their flexibility and their ability to think on their feet to develop winning tactics as negotiations progress.

One role winners should never adopt – or be pushed into – is that of the 'enemy', even if it is a role their opposite seems to have assigned to them. In *Negotiate for What you Want*, Henry Calero and Bob Oskam suggest that the best way to tackle this is to make it clear that you view your opposite as a potential ally – your 'oppo' in fact – and that it is the problem and not your opposite which is the source of any difficulty which has to be resolved.

This of course is where winning with words comes in, because as they move into the negotiations proper, winners will choose words which will make their attitudes – and needs – apparent at an early stage. Making one's needs apparent – asking for things, in other words – is something winners should be careful to do and it's amazing how many people in negotiating situations forget the childhood cliché to the effect that 'if you don't ask, you don't get'.

In negotiations this could result in protracted discussions, at the end of which one party says, 'Good Heavens! So what you really wanted all along was X? We were certain you wanted Y, which is impossible, but if you give us Z, of course you can have X.'

WINNING WITH QUESTIONS

It's worth remembering that friendly questioning can often help us to establish what it is our opposite really wants, after which it becomes a matter of bargaining.

Before the evolution of language, if individuals or groups wanted something and could not come to an immediate agreement, their choice was either to flee or to fight. Now, thanks to words, we can negotiate, which involves using personality and persuasion to talk our way through to a mutually satisfactory result. Winners know that in negotiations of all kinds – *polite, persistent persuasion pays.*

It is of course only polite, if you are the host team, to provide your opposites with a comfortable, efficiently arranged and equipped conference room with tables at the right height and so on – not forgetting such details as getting a woman member of your team or organisation to show the women opposites how to find the ladies' loo. Male winners may find that politeness and courtesy shown to women opposites helps negotiations run smoothly as women in such situations often adopt a more formal, even prickly, manner than the men, simply because they expect – often with good reason – to be patronised and put upon.

Women winners, on the other hand, when faced with women opposites may decide to play the 'sister' card, which can be done by merely raising an eyebrow if any of the male opposites reveal, say, tendencies towards male chauvinism.

It is polite, too, to provide your opposites with basic information about your own team and to make introductions if necessary. Winners remember that moving into the conference room or sitting down at the table is not the equivalent of taking the gloves off or unsheathing the foils and that *politeness pays* throughout.

This is not to say that you can't start negotiations with a verbal punch to make sure you have your opposites' full attention. Asking for three times X when you will be prepared to settle for X is a basic and well tried example of this ploy.

ACCENTUATE THE POSITIVE

After the punch, if any, it's time to accentuate the *positive* with an up-beat tone, an assurance of flexibility and an underlying theme – stated or implied – that 'We know what we want and we think we know what you want. We'd like you to clarify your requirements so that together we can come to an agreement which will benefit all concerned.'

Also implied is 'We are all of us good negotiators – good game-players – who know what we want and one thing we want is for everyone concerned to leave feeling we have had a constructive day of hard negotiating which has not only achieved a satisfactory agreement but has left us better friends than we were before the negotiations began.

'None of us would be here if we didn't want something and, in return for a little goodwill in giving us at least some of what we want, we will try to see that *you* get what you want.'

WINNERS ARE NEGOTIATORS WHO LIKE TO SAY 'YES'

At the height of the Cold War, Soviet negotiators became famous for their intransigence, which made certain that almost everyone in the West knew at least one word of Russian – 'Niet!'

This could not be described as winning with words and in fact, at the time, the atmosphere of most East–West negotiations was so daunting to the Russians' opposites that the Westerners usually went home feeling that a few extra billions for arms would be money well spent.

Winning negotiators use words which signal that they are prepared and even willing to say 'yes' and that, knowing that their opposites are asking, 'What's in it for us?' they are prepared to answer, 'Well, let's see, shall we? We can probably work something out.'

This attitude avoids the sort of arrogance which can kill negotiations and which frequently expresses itself in condescending language more appropriate for a group of medieval barons addressing the peasantry than a discussion between equals.

LEAVE THE HIGH HORSE IN THE STABLE

We like the term 'plenipotentiary arrogance' for the near madness which can affect the nicest people when they are negotiating on behalf of large numbers of members or constituents, often representing considerable collective power.

Winners learn to recognise and suppress this sort of arrogance in themselves and to make allowances for it in others. They know – if they are not just negotiating on their own behalf – that, while it is essential to keep the people for whom they are negotiating in mind at all times, 'plenipotentiary arrogance' can make them prickly and insufferable as well as endangering the outcome of the negotiations.

NEGOTIATING IS FUN

Like many other things in life, if you are good at it negotiating is highly enjoyable, so much so that few top negotiators would wish to give it up.

Negotiating may imply 'not leisure', but the fact that, say, a professional golfer's games are 'not leisure' doesn't prevent him from enjoying them, and winning negotiators can turn a conference room into a comfort zone, filled with the buzzing excitement of people who are determined to get things done and perhaps echo the 'Nobody sleeps while I'm on' boast of the old vaudeville comedian. After all, you can't persuade someone who is asleep or 'switched off', or produce counter-arguments if you are in the middle of a daydream.

Winners with words will need all their skill and attention if they are to appreciate their opposites' choice of words and the tone in which they are delivered, especially as they have to decide whether they are speaking in 'clear' or in 'code'.

BREAKING THE CODES

Some negotiators employ complicated tactics and convoluted reasoning on the lines of 'If they know that we know that they know that we know . . .' and introduce further elements of confusion by speaking in code when they could go into caucus.

On the whole, winners with words should neither engage in nor worry about this sort of thing, but should endeavour to keep things simple and straightforward – even if the simplicity, being bankable, may on occasions hide a bare minimum of guile.

What winners must watch for is 'meta-talk', a term used by negotiators to describe 'speaking in terms which disguise a hidden meaning'. Something like, 'We know that you will appreciate the proposals we are about to make,' for example, could really mean, 'We are going to use an attractive fly and see if you take the hook.'

Some politicians use a great deal of meta-talk – which

accounts for the cynical expression of those who have to listen to them and filter what they are saying to discover what they really mean.

The counter to meta-talk is usually a frown of 'honest' puzzlement, accompanied perhaps by a polite request for clarification.

PRACTICAL WINNING

Seek out a couple of prime examples of meta-talk – the political sections of newspapers are usually full of them – and translate to reveal the speaker's real meaning. Winners with words will find that with practice, especially when they are reading as opposed to hearing meta-talk, their minds provide a running translation, which can be as amusing as it is instructive.

NEGOTIATING FOR MONEY

In one way or another, negotiating permeates the whole of our lives, and both informal negotiations and the formal type we've been discussing can be about many things. However, one specialised form of negotiating in which winners with words can show their mettle – and make anything from a good living to a fortune – is important enough to be considered separately. It is called selling and usually involves negotiating to exchange goods or services for money.

Winning Words

If you think you'll lose, you've lost,
For out in the world you'll find
Success begins with the will to win:
It's all in the state of mind.

It's not good enough to have a good mind, the main
thing is to use it well!
  René Descartes

Don't tell me how hard you work.
Tell me how much you get done.
  James Ling

It doesn't matter whether you win or lose – until you
lose.

8

WORDS THAT WIN
SALES

One word that, perhaps more than any other, can help salespeople to become winners is the word 'sell' itself, because all they need do is go back to the origins of the word to discover that selling is an occupation of which anyone can be justly proud.

Of course they already know this to be true but, sadly, the snowball effect, which adds layers of meaning to words over the years, has done 'selling' no good whatsoever and the word has acquired distinct overtones of amorality and chicanery, so much so that salesmen, tired of being tarred with the same brush as their mountebank forerunners, have changed into 'consultants' or promoted themselves to 'executives'. In fact, selling is merely a specialised form of negotiation in which goods or services are transferred from one person to another in exchange for money and is a perfectly honourable occupation.

This becomes apparent when we realise that the word 'sell' derives originally from the Latin 'consilium', meaning to advise, so that all those salespeople who have 'Counsellor' or 'Advisor' on their business cards are absolutely right – even though linguistic nicety may not have been their first consideration.

Wise counselling is what a winner who wishes to sell should undertake, and it is also what validates – more than any course or examination – the claim of salesmanship's practitioners to belong to a profession.

WE ARE ALL SELLING

Just as most of us negotiate throughout the whole of our lives, almost all of us spend a lot of time trying to sell something to somebody and the distinction between professional salesmen and others becomes blurred. However, all selling is initiated, continued and finalised in words, and for winners the principles of selling are the same whether they are selling an idea, a barrel of flour, a million pounds' worth of widgets – or themselves.

A winning sale is a bargain in every sense of the word, in which both parties to the deal have won and know they have won. Those salespeople who believe that 'a sale is a sale' no matter how it is obtained, and that all that matters is the signature on the order form, forget the implicit contract behind every sales transaction – that the salesman in his role as wise counsellor must make sure that every customer is a satisfied customer. Enlightened self-interest dictates that this should be the case and even 'hit and run' salesmen will find that they lose by trying to make deals which leave the customer a loser, if only when they take into account their large number of cancellations.

CONMEN LOSE: SALESMEN WIN

In some ways, like the word 'sell', the word 'honest' has acquired a pejorative sense, so that 'to be honest' has become a conman's catchphrase which screams at customers that they are about to be duped. The implication that the salesman is about to abandon a life of deception makes the phrase as laughable as those salesmen's oaths, which make much of the lives of babies and mothers and are almost always sworn by salesmen who are childless orphans.

This is a pity because, when it comes to selling, honesty really is the best way to sell a policy – or indeed anything else.

Unfortunately, many salesmen seem determined to believe their bad press and behave accordingly, deriving a perverse pleasure from talking about their 'cons', even though their actions are usually more underhand than illegal.

On the other hand, we know of one man who lost his business through no fault of his own and took a 'commission only' job selling sets of children's books. Strangely enough, he discovered that he was not only good at the job but enjoyed it, mainly because he realised that the books, had they been available when he was a schoolboy, would have helped him with his own O-levels.

Putting the case in this way, to parents of children who had just begun secondary school courses, enabled him to make so many sales he was soon asked to take over a team of salespeople and was astonished to find that, even though many of them were experienced, they were achieving only poor figures and had very high cancellation rates. He was even more astonished to discover that the reason for their failure was a 'conman' approach which began with the easily disproved claim that they had been 'sent by the school'. There was apparently no end to the lies they were prepared to tell when attempting to sell items which people were happy to buy when they were sold honestly. In the end self-interest converted most of them to the 'honest' method, but a few quit rather than change their ways.

THE CASE OF THE HONEST ESTATE AGENT

Honesty is the best policy and sometimes, when even tougher tactics are called for, candour verging on the suicidal can win the day.

For instance, at a time when his estate agent colleagues had perfected a language of their own in which, for example, 'would repay attention' meant 'totally derelict' and 'period' meant 'no loo, no electricity – and totally derelict', London agent Roy Brooks embarked on a sales campaign of seemingly self-destructive honesty.

His ads, on the lines of 'Artist owners are asking far too much for this ghastly example of Victorian Gothic, largely destroyed by huge family and assorted dogs – but they will haggle' soon became collectors' items and sold houses by the hundred.

Winning salespeople find that this sort of 'warts and all' honesty about the product – provided they can be genuinely enthusiastic about it in most respects – pays, because most potential customers don't know as much about the product as the salesman, so what they are in fact buying is – the salesman.

WINNING SALES AT THE BREAKFAST TABLE

The Germans have a saying to the effect that *'Gut begonnen ist halb gewonnen'* – or 'Well begun is half won' – and this is certainly the case with salesmen, as the people who share their homes can send them out of the house feeling either like losers about to try conclusions with a cold and hostile world or winners off to make friends and influence cheque books.

This is where winners with words pick up dividends for having made their homes into comfort zones and, while winners will have a great deal more going for them than a family that gives them confidence along with their corn-flakes, a winning family can give salespeople the winning attitude that good sales managers try desperately to instil.

So important is attitude that a winner could almost certainly dress like a tramp, forget his sales kit, make every mistake in the manual and still finish up with a sale. However, doing things correctly, as well as having the right attitude, makes selling easier – which is the way winners like things.

ALL PSYCHED-UP AND LOTS OF PLACES TO GO

Of course, the best attitude in the world is no use without potential customers and winners always seem to be busy. Not that they are overworked – that's not the winner's way – but if the phone rings it's usually for them, and even if they are not professional salesmen they always seem to be at the centre of one of those networks of bargains, helping hands and useful contacts which are such a large part of winning.

The winner's contacts book contains not only the names of his customers, and potential customers, but is a treasury of all kinds of other contacts, ranging from the plumber who will always turn out to the man who repairs Super Widgets in his spare time.

Naturally, winners are generous with advice, contacts and time – they are the first people you turn to if you need help – but if they think at all about the activity they are generating, they would probably admit that in addition to behaving like a good friend they are also exposing themselves to the danger of making sales.

PRACTICAL WINNING

Start a contacts book, even if you are not a professional salesman. If you are, make sure that in addition to business addresses your book contains the sort of information your customers and potential customers might find useful.

If you are a professional, ask yourself if you are using your contacts book to full advantage. Are you asking for recommendations or just waiting for them? Are you mining the newspapers and other publications for leads? Are you client-spotting among the firms' vans that have you pinned down in traffic jams?

EVERY SALESMAN AND HIS CUSTOMERS WANT SOMETHING

At first sight the sales situation seems to be the most cut-and-dried application possible of the Everybody Wants Something rule, with the salesman wanting to make a sale and the prospect either wanting what is being sold or wanting to hang on to his money.

In fact, the potential customer may have agreed to see the salesman for any one or several of a number of reasons, including a desire to spend what should be working time in chatting, a wish to exercise power, a need for an excuse to spend money he intended spending anyway – or even a genuine wish to be thoroughly counselled before buying. Applying the Everyone Wants Something rule to determine exactly what it is that prospects want can save wasting a great deal of time.

WHAT DO YE LACK?

Building up an intelligence system of passive and active contacts is one way of winning sales with words, but equally important is identifying the needs of potential customers. In many cases people do not realise that they want something until it is offered to them, and the salesman is perfectly within his rights to display his wares to their best advantage.

In this connection the medieval street vendors who cried, 'What do ye lack?' rather than 'What can I sell you?' were already in the business of winning with words, by identifying their customers' needs.

Nowadays the multi-million-pound advertising and public relations industries attempt to win with words by bringing ideas and products to the attention of potential customers and, while a fraction of the output of these professionals is frankly awful, there are so many examples of well written words and first-class ideas that winners can learn a great deal from analysing them and discovering how their effects are obtained.

Identifying the need

GETTING THEIR ATTENTION

Remember the story of the man who was hitting his donkey and told the old lady who remonstrated with him that he would stop beating it and speak to it nicely as soon he had got its attention?

Of course, we're not suggesting that you beat potential customers but it is essential that you get their attention before you try to put your message across. This means that the first few lines of your brochure or sales letter should shock, excite, arouse interest and tell the story of how your product can improve your potential customer's life or business.

Don't forget that in a communication situation where most people shout loudly the winning move is either to shout louder still or to whisper something interesting, and that what interests most people, above all things, is their own concerns. In fact most people are so self-orientated that a whisper of 'Fire!' is more effective than a cry of 'Help!'

However, attention-getters need not be all that blatant and a winner can command attention merely by deviating from the established form of words. We know of one top copy writer, for example, who was anxious to bring her professional writing skills to the attention of potential clients – people she knew were being bombarded with mail by other talented writers. Of course she could have sought attention by including glamour pictures of herself with her mail shots or by wildly exaggerating her achievements. Instead, she wrote a fairly modest letter summarising the type of writing she had done and for whom but, instead of the formal salutation, began 'Hi! My name is Beverly and I love to write . . .' which, since she'd not only aroused interest but proved she could do the job she was pitching for, brought in enough clients to set her business on the road to expansion.

THE DAY OF THE SOPHISTICATED CUSTOMER

There was a time when anyone with the brains of a parrot could be taught to sell and, even today, salesmen who learn a professionally written script by heart are bound to meet the odd person who has been waiting to buy double glazing or a time-share holiday home. This is winning with other people's words and while winners are pleased to learn – and not too proud to borrow – they prefer to develop their own winning words and style.

Fortunately today's customers are better educated and more sophisticated than was once the case and often enjoy having things sold to them, providing the salesman fulfils the unspoken contract to provide information, wise counsel and perhaps a modicum of entertainment in exchange for a hearing.

Salesmen who are able to win with words, unlike the aggressive types, the conmen and the snake-oil merchants, rarely have the depressing experience of having their orders cancelled. This is because, if a winner with words sells you a racing greyhound with a wooden leg, you will have bought it knowing full well that what you were really getting was – a pet.

'NO' IS A WINNING WORD

One reason winners with words are able to make more firm sales than many of their colleagues is that they are not afraid of some of the things that give many salesmen night-mares – one of which is the word 'No'. Fundamentally there is no reason for the paralysing effects of this word, unless they derive from childhood memories of negatives that sounded like parental rejection.

Winners know that even they 'can't win them all' and

realise that, while a knee-jerk reaction 'No', or a 'No' based on lack of information, is a challenge calling for polite persistence, a genuine 'No' can save them a great deal of time that can be profitably spent elsewhere. Not only that, but they will probably be able to change the 'No' into a 'Let's have another chat about this on such and such a date', together with a few recommendations to people more likely to come up with an immediate 'Yes'.

Winner salesmen hear the word 'No' less often than their colleagues, mainly because they expect a 'Yes', which gives their whole attitude and vocabulary a positive cast so that – without soliciting agreement every few minutes as some sales trainers advise – they are in fact eliciting agreement all along the line.

Winners expect to win because they feel a genuine mission to put their product into the hands of people who will enjoy or benefit from it, they know enough about the product to act as genuine counsellors, they regard every potential new customer as a new friend and can turn every sales situation into a comfort zone.

They do not despise their customers or potential customers as 'punters' and 'peasants', or change into unctuous 'grovellers' and 'cringers' at the drop of a note of finality.

We are not all that happy about the use of the word 'prospect' – with its hint of fossicking for gold teeth – to refer to a potential customer, but the word is compact and useful enough to have gained general acceptance. By contrast the word 'customer' tells us a great deal about how winners should go about selling, as it comes via Old French from the Latin 'consuescere', meaning 'to grow accustomed to', a splendid way of describing the process by which winners use words to turn prospects into long-term friends – and customers.

MAGIC WORDS

Selling is not an adversarial situation; the potential customer is not an enemy but a human being who may well become a friend and who, like all human beings, enjoys hearing his own name and being verbally stroked, likes hearing the magic words *you, your* and *yours*, and almost certainly will not object if you express your genuine admiration of his possessions and good taste.

Winners, unless their product is grossly over-priced – in which case they should be going through their 'parachute' files to find a new job – don't worry too much about price. Unless it's a genuine 'can't afford' or 'don't have the budget' – both of which objections can often be transformed into a 'will be able to afford' – most customers don't decide to buy or not on price, and the winner with words, having found out almost without trying that the customer *can* afford, will have made the price seem trivial or perhaps, as in the case of the recent beer advertisement, the product 'reassuringly expensive'.

Thinking of your new friend as a 'customer', rather than a 'prospect', helps maintain the right attitude as you move towards that bogey of many salesmen, the close – or the order-signing stage – when winners simply ask for the business in the workmanlike manner of someone recognising a foregone conclusion. 'We'll just get the paperwork out of the way, shall we?' could fit the bill, with perhaps a variation of the classic 'choice' close, like 'We did agree on *blue* widgets, didn't we?' or 'Do you think a hundred will be enough?'

Magic words can even enable winners with words to by-pass the dreaded close altogether, because winners don't say 'When I sell' or 'When you buy' or even 'When you own', although the last is on the right lines. Instead, winners with words, assuming a sale, will say something like 'As the owner of . . .' and, having picked up assent signals throughout the sale, will have gone past the close so that the actual signing of the order is a mere formality between friends.

Winners are also happy to stay with customers for a few minutes at the end of the sales 'courtship', because the easiest way to make people feel they have been screwed rather than wooed is to get straight out of bed and go home.

Winners know that their presence is needed during that curious after-sales period during which the customer is filled with a mixture of euphoria and buyer's remorse, a state of mind which often includes an element of 'Do you still respect me?' Winners provide every reassurance, including a telephone number and a promise to call at a specific future date – 'to make sure you're getting the best out of your Widget Six'.

Of course, they make use of both the euphoria and the follow-up call to obtain recommendations from the 'proud owner', but at the same time their assurances, and the fact that they *do* keep in touch as they promised, fulfil the final clause in the implicit contract which requires that both sides finish up winners.

CUSTOMERS IN THE COMPANY

Winners with words will have appreciated that almost everything we've said about selling so far applies equally to non-professional selling situations – like selling ideas or selling ourselves – and that winning sales behaviour like respecting the customer, gaining attention, giving good service and so on, can help us in our everyday lives.

To the winner with words everyone is a potential 'customer' who can be wooed with words and made into a fellow winner by polite, persistent persuasion, and nowhere is this more the case than in the workplace where our 'customers' are the people who work in the departments which we or our group supply or service.

In his Industrial Motivation work Nick Thornely makes a point of explaining that although in any organisation it is the ultimate purchaser of the product who pays the wages of everyone, from office boy to managing director, it is the intermediate 'customers' within the firm who make everything possible and who should be treated exactly as though they were paying cash for every transaction. In this way, instead of thinking of our colleagues in other departments – or at the next desk – as 'those useless blighters in packing' or 'those idiots in the typing pool' we begin thinking of them as valued customers for our services who, as self-interest demands, should be wooed, stroked and sold to with as much care and enthusiasm as any other paying customer. Thinking about the workplace in this way will not only improve 'customer relations' between departments but will help maintain and even improve the quality of the goods or services we offer. After all, if we fail to sell to an outside customer there will usually be others to take their place, but if we ruin customer relationships in our own organisation by providing inferior products and services, or by failing to win with words, we could be stuck with some dissatisfied 'customers' for the rest of our working lives.

PRACTICAL WINNING

If you are not a professional salesperson, have a look at a couple of books on selling and see if there are any more sales techniques you could usefully employ to win with words within your own organisation. We recommend the following published by Mercury: Michael Beer's *The Joy of Selling*, John Fenton's *Close! Close! Close!* and Peter Amis and Jackie Head's *The Salesman's Handbook* or *The Saleswoman's Handbook* – whichever you prefer!

If you *are* a professional, ask yourself if you are one of those few salesmen who leave their charm and their salesmanship at the gate when they get back to their own organisation or perhaps, worse still, when they get home. Winners with words behave like winners, and make others feel like winners, wherever they happen to be.

MAKING FRIENDS AND INFLUENCING SALES

Because being a winner with words, especially in sales situations, means being sensitive to other people's wants and moods, as well as being able to respond to them, good salespeople not only make friends easily but also make good friends.

Of course, the winning salesman knows, if he stops to think about it, that the receptionist or the office boy he chats to as he goes about his business can not only be helpful today but could become the managing director of tomorrow, so that most of his actions have an element of enlightened self-interest. He even knows that he's more likely to make sales if people are glad to see him.

However, as he walks through the door with a pleasant smile and a cheerful word for everyone he meets, he's more likely to be thinking how amazing it is that anyone should pay him for visiting his friends and making new ones – and it shows.

Winning Words

Show me a successful person and I will show you a salesman. The fact is, we are all selling one way or another.
  Richard Denny

Do not complicate simplicity by simplifying that which is complicated.

'There are no easy answers!'

(There is always the tendency to seek the superficial, attractive answers rather than to grind away at finding more durable solutions.)
  Sir Denys Henderson (chairman, ICI PLC).

9

THE MARTIAL ARTS
OF WORDPLAY

Medieval knights, Japanese samurai, and the rest of the legendary warriors of the past had to undergo years of intensive training in the use of weaponry before being sent into combat, so it seems absurd that in these days, when so many of life's battles are fought with words, most of us are sent out into the world with little or no training in their use.

Words are weapons which can be used for both defence and attack and winners with words should be able to handle them in both situations with all the control of the skilled practitioner.

Fortunately, using words in this particular way is merely an advanced form of winning with words, so that much of what we have been considering up to this point will be useful and, just as the home makes an ideal place to learn the art of general conversation, it's also a training ground on which fledgling winners can try out their weaponry and the more mature can test their skills. There, like children play-fighting with wooden swords, winners with words can learn to use verbal weapons without anyone risking much more than the equivalent of a bang on the knuckles.

Curiously, one of the first weapons children learn how to use, perhaps because it is as deceptively simple as language itself, is one of the most powerful in the winner's armoury – humour.

HUMOUR IN THE HOME

Children soon learn that an angry parent can be disarmed by a well aimed wisecrack – a lesson which should stand them in good stead for the rest of their lives. They learn, too, that not everyone will share their sense of humour and that it is quite possible to 'die of an unfortunate remark' if they fail to read the mood of the person who is the target of their jokes.

Some girls, the fortunate ones, learn to use humour to defend themselves and acquire a weapon which may well be as useful to them in the still largely male-dominated outside world as a karate course.

Adults should learn to refrain from using the full power of their humour on those less skilled than themselves and realise that, ideally, humorous exchanges within the family, even if they begin with people laughing at each other, should end with them laughing *with* each other in what is a win–win outcome.

Domestic humour is based on shared background and experience; it should be used not destructively, or even abrasively, but as an intimacy reinforcer, full of secret codes and allusions which will help maintain the winning home as a comfort zone.

Moving outside the home, children learn – usually at school – that while it can be a moderately winning move to adopt the role of group jester, this is only the case if the jester is known to carry a dagger in his motley and that, while being the target of other people's jokes may provide entrée into a group, it does not always make it a comfort zone for the person concerned.

Learning to use humour in the home can help us to win with words in pubs, clubs and even in the street, often by defusing situations that might otherwise turn nasty, but it is in the workplace that humour and other verbal weapons come into their own.

HUMOUR IN THE WORKPLACE

In the workplace, winners can use humour to deal with the ubiquitous Jobsworth clan and all the others who like to say 'No', as well as to defend themselves against attack and to create workplace family groups which function as headquarters and bases.

Women – who know that outside the home and the workplace it's sometimes possible to use humour to avoid physical confrontation – can use it as the ideal weapon against many forms of sexual harassment.

We know of one case in which an office lecher, who made the working lives of a dozen or so women a little hell with his suggestive remarks, was completely defeated by a constant barrage of humour on the lines of 'Oh, here comes the lovely Ron. What does the little dear want today?'

Humour can also be used in the workplace as a weapon to force through projects which might otherwise get lost in the hierarchy and to spark off ideas in the play-fight atmosphere of brain-storming sessions. Here winners with words must be careful to joust only with their peers as a carelessly wielded wisecrack can kill someone else's idea stone dead. Mind you, if humour aimed downwards can hurt, humour aimed upwards can be lethal – to the career of the humorist – and many a promotion has foundered on a joke about the boss that was too good not to repeat. This is why winners take care that any wisecracks they make outside their workplace family group are ones they wouldn't mind seeing pinned up in the executive dining room with their name attached.

A FEW HUMOROUS WORDS

In the workplace as elsewhere, style is important and some winners are able to 'get away with' more than others, so much so that a 'licensed jester' can often steer meetings in the direction he wishes them to go, by the use of humour alone.

Professional comedians, of course, are the archetypal licensed jesters. Bob Monkhouse generously invites his readers to make use of his jokes when called upon to 'say a few words', but the difficulty is that when he comes out with something like: 'Well, we all know the chairman doesn't really like to drink – it's just something to do while he gets drunk' or 'What can I say about our sales director? He's been called cold, rude, self-centred and egotistical. But that's just his family's opinion,' even in print, you can hear Bob delivering the lines and getting a hearty laugh from everyone, including the victims. This is because Bob is not only a licensed jester but a professional licensed jester whose style most people recognise and they would probably feel cheated if he left a speaking engagement without having delivered a few cheerful insults.

Not everyone can get away with using humour in this way and winners should try out premeditated jokes on a captive audience like a partner and, if possible, rehearse 'off-the-cuff' wisecracks in their minds before delivering them. Winners who have mastered this trick of listening to themselves before they speak will find this invaluable, especially in meetings and negotiations.

PRAISE THE BARD AND PASS THE AMMUNITION

Of course it's all very well talking about wordplay and the way winners use words as weapons – but where do they get all their ammunition? The answer is, of course, anywhere they can, adding to their armoury by stealing, borrowing, adapting and by conjuring verbal missiles out of thin air.

Many winners – like most comedians – find it useful to keep a notebook in which to write any wisecracks, put-downs and other examples of verbal weaponry that take their fancy, and this sort of borrowing has a long history. There is, for example, the classic story involving one of the greatest of British wits, Oscar Wilde, who once said admiringly, of a savage line delivered by the painter Whistler, 'I wish I'd said that,' to which the artist replied sweetly, 'You will, Oscar, you will!'

Wilde and Whistler are both fertile sources of verbal weaponry, as are more modern conversation-stoppers like Dorothy Parker, and it's still possible to pick up a few goodies by trawling through Shakespeare. Then there are theatre critics, like the one who wrote of one actress that she 'glowed like a forty-watt bulb' while another 'ran the gamut of emotions from A to B'.

There's no shortage of verbal facilities to choose from but, alas, many of the best ones are too well known to be used without at least a wry smile of acknowledgement.

Another way in which to use all this marvellous material is to adapt it, which can be done in most cases fairly simply with a pun or some other sort of twist of the original. Almost any well known phrase, saying, or song title can be used in this way and, especially when the sayings are clichés or over-quoted gems like much of Shakespeare, changing a word or two not only gives them freshness but often highlights the word magic of the original which has been obscured by over-use.

In verbal duelling, an expert can sometimes persuade his opposite that he is about to be attacked with a hoary old saying or cliché, only to fool him in the last split second with a flick of the uvula which turns the feint into an almost unstoppable attack, calling for an instant riposte – a word which, incidentally, is now used much more of verbal fencing than of swordplay.

This sort of duelling needs practice, but it is the sort of exercise which can be undertaken 'by consenting adults in the privacy of their own home' – an example, incidentally, of how words can be given new force by using them out of their original context.

PRACTICAL WINNING

Write down a few clichés, toothless old saws or jokes long past their tell-by date, and think how you might burnish them into usable verbal weaponry by changing a word or two or transposing a couple of letters. One of our favourites, for instance, was coined by a Fleet Street editor who put an instruction on the notice board reading: 'In future, editorial staff will avoid clichés like the plague.'

Don't worry if some of your efforts sound familiar. 'Cutting the whole of Act Two would be the kindest cut of all' is one we've just thought up while day-dreaming about the theatre critic's enviable licence to be bitchy, but we wouldn't like to bet that it has never been used before.

DAY-DREAMING AND OTHER FORMS OF HARD WORK

Day-dreaming, word association and stream of consciousness, are ways in which winners with words can let their mental computers do the work. Many experts believe that every word we have ever seen or heard is permanently registered among the multi-million synapses and switches of our brains which means that, while we are drifting off into reverie, our one-armed bandit minds can scroll through hundreds of thousands of words and are bound to come up with a few jackpots.

Undirected day-dreaming of this sort is enjoyable and can produce useful results, but there are ways of giving our mental computers a nudge in the direction we wish them to go and of getting our minds to make curious sideways leaps into the Alice in Wonderland world of lateral thinking.

Word association is also a way in which we can train for verbal duelling, until every phrase we hear triggers a response which is then submitted to a split-second analysis so that only the most appropriate are spoken.

Writing gives us a chance to slow down this process and to be even more selective, but winners with words have to learn to do this sort of thinking on their feet.

One way of appreciating how the process works is to listen to youngsters who have just found out about the word connections their minds can make and are trying them out without any attempt at selection.

A fractionally more adult way of illustrating this particular mental ability is to play a favourite schoolboy game which involves adding the phrase 'as the actress said to the bishop' to everything that is said. This is often the adolescent's first introduction to the *double entendre* and they find it remarkable how much of what we say is capable of a sexual interpretation – as the actress said to the bishop.

Older people will get fed up with this after a while – as the actress said to the bishop – but the *double entendre* is the basis of much adult humour and a trenchant weapon which can be used, say, to throw a meeting completely off balance if someone who is being pompous about making a serious point comes up with a piece of unintentional lewdery.

In fact, unintentional *double entendres* of this sort are so common that one Fleet Street newspaper found retirement employment for a particularly filthy-minded former sub-editor who was given the job of reading every word of the paper before publication, a belly laugh from his corner of the editorial floor being enough to kill the paragraph which triggered his peculiar sense of humour.

Winners – especially if they are to listen to themselves formulating sentences – will try to avoid double meanings of this sort in speech and will go through all letters and written work with the possibility of unconscious humour in mind. However, they can never eradicate all such unintentional jokes and 'Sod's Law' will ensure that they occur at the worst possible times when the only thing winners can do is to laugh along with the rest and pretend they meant it all along.

PRACTICAL WINNING

Try playing the 'as the actress said to the bishop' game, either in your mind or with someone with a fairly broad sense of humour.

Read through a newspaper – a local one could well be the best as they are probably short of evil-minded staff – and pick out any examples of double meanings. You might even find it salutary to go through your own recent correspondence to see if anything capable of being misinterpreted has crept in.

FREUDIAN SLEEPS

Sex seems to trigger off verbal association more easily than any other topic but, if you have the sort of mind that almost automatically registers a naughty dream as a 'Freudian sleep', you should have no trouble with other ways of persuading your brain to make useful sideways leaps and provide you with an inexhaustible supply of verbal armament. One way to see how this works, and at the same time get in some useful practice, is to take the first word that comes into your head – which could be, say, 'Sparrow'; the word this suggests might be 'Hawk', followed by 'Moth', followed by 'Ball', and so on. It's useful to use a tape recorder for this as, in the first instance, writing leaves too much time for conscious thought.

Winners with words find that, with practice, this sort of lateral association becomes second nature, so that all speech and writing that comes their way is subjected to it – in addition to all the other forms of analysis, for content, sincerity and the like, which the brain performs automatically.

In the case of verbal fencing the word associations made in this way can reveal gaps in the other person's defences and enable us to exploit them. For example, the word 'husband' can easily trigger off the word 'wife' – which perhaps gave rise to Churchill's riposte when Nancy Astor told him, 'If you were my husband, Winston, I would poison your brandy,' to the effect that, 'If you were my wife, Nancy – I'd drink it.'

It can also be used very effectively in self-defence, as in 'You're nothing but a crook', to which the reply might be 'You are absolutely right and I do sometimes feel as though my only function in life is to herd a flock of silly sheep.'

Of course, lateral thinking has a much more important role than suggesting put-downs and wisecracks because, as a fundamental part of the creative process, it can help us to win with words by coming up with completely new ideas – perhaps, say, in the middle of a meeting.

It has a role, too, in our handling of correspondence of

all types, where – keeping the Everybody Wants Something rule in mind – the writer's choice of vocabulary can provide useful clues to what they are really trying to say or what they are trying to conceal, as well as perhaps triggering off a creative response.

LEARNING TO THINK LATERALLY

Crossword puzzles are a useful way of learning to think laterally and to use the responses triggered off by word association. In general, the ones that look more difficult are preferable to the simpler-seeming variety as they tend to be fairer, with less chance of ambiguity, but beginners should try puzzles they find they can solve. Following the same crossword in a particular daily newspaper often enables us to get to know how the puzzle creator's mind works and to make the same verbal connections as he does.

In much the same way partners, and people who work together, often develop a rapport based on being able to pick up each other's associations, even before they are verbalised, and this is particularly helpful in problem-solving and brain-storming sessions.

Couples, especially, those who have been together for some time, learn to use unspoken words in reply to the other person's spoken ones, finding that a raised eyebrow, a knowing smile or arms firmly akimbo can be a perfect riposte. This technique, of course, can be used as a weapon in verbal jousting of all sorts and can, for example, be seen to advantage in the televised sessions of the House of Commons, where the body language of MPs listening to members of the opposing parties tends to be extremely eloquent.

Using body language to help win with words in this way can be very effective, especially as 'raised eyebrows' or 'feigned yawn' rarely appear in the minutes, but it can also be extremely annoying and should be used relatively sparingly.

WINNING WEAPONRY

So far we've looked at just one or two weapons which can be used to joust with words. But there are many more available, and ways in which words can be used to wound range from the mocking taps of banter and raillery to the harsh blows of ridicule and derision.

Words can turn an opponent into a laughing stock or persuade others to regard him with repugnance, disgust and even loathing.

Words can belittle, criticise, vilify, lampoon and traduce and be used to damn with faint praise.

Words can demean, degrade, and dishonour; they can even cause people to take their own lives, so don't tell anyone who has ever been verbally flayed that 'words can never hurt' them – they can!

The point is that while winners with words *can* hurt people, they rarely do so, because like a martial arts expert they have learned to control their power.

PRACTICAL WINNING

Think back to any time when you were hurt by another person's intentionally cruel or carelessly insensitive words. Perhaps something of the sort happened recently, or maybe you have to go back to your childhood to remember a time when someone was really hurtful, but playing back the scene in your mind is not only cathartic but a useful reminder of how much the winning rule of 'Do As You Would Be Done By' applies to winning with words.

A BLACK BELT IN BADINAGE

Winners with words almost never use their full powers, but there are some verbal battles which are like street fights in which even a master may be compelled to employ a few crippling blows.

However, in the main, verbal contests, whether jousting or for real, can be compared with the exercise of martial arts in both their 'hard' and 'soft' forms, ranging from semi-formal practice sessions to the rigid forms of actual competition.

Winners show the same respect to their opposites as that which judokas express in formal if wary bows. Then comes the 'feeling-out' phase in which contestants try to discover each other's strengths and weaknesses, followed by throws, counters and rapid recoveries.

Then, in the final phase, the opposing 'player' is either thrown or 'pinned down' – the technical term is interesting – helpless but unhurt, and then released with the equivalent of more mutual bowing.

The comparison holds good for all forms of martial art from tai kwan do to karate and kendo – from the subtle to the not so subtle – and winners with words can learn from their practitioners to respect their opposites and to realise that a Brown Belt in browbeating or a Black Belt in badinage implies a definite responsibility not to abuse their ability when up against a less skilled opponent.

More important perhaps than any of these similarities is the fact that many martial arts theorists believe it is possible for the true masters to tap into the mysterious forces of their mind, their body and perhaps even of nature itself. Some winners with words are able to do this and all of us are capable of appreciating and using a little of that mysterious power of words which combines music and magic.

Winning Words

Nothing in the world can take the place of persistence. Talent will not; nothing is more common than unsuccessful men with great talent. Genius will not; unrewarded genius is almost a proverb. Education will not; the world is full of educated derelicts. Persistence, determination alone are omnipotent!
Calvin Coolidge

'The best is the enemy of the good.'

(I have seen so many business situations where people go on seeking the ultimate solution, that the moment for action has gone by and they have lost the opportunity. It is better to move fast with a good solution than to seek perfection.)
Sir John Harvey-Jones (chairman, Parallax Enterprises Ltd)

Success is a journey and not a destination

10

WONDERFUL WAYS TO
WIN WITH WORDS

Who? What? Where? and When? are among the shortest words in the English language and the most effective – especially in the workplace. They are the four 'Ws' every aspiring journalist learns must be included in his story if he is to avoid, for example, writing a powerful piece about a disastrous fire and omitting to say 'where' it happened. They are words that should be in the minds of everyone who prepares a speech, attends a meeting or puts pen to paper. They are words which can help us to win.

'I have six honest serving men,' runs Rudyard Kipling's poem, 'They taught me all I knew; their names are What and Why and When and How and Where and Who.'

Of course, one can have too much of even a splendid mnemonic like alliteration, but it is difficult to resist asserting that Who? What? Where? When? and Why? are Wonderful Ways to Win With Words.

THE FIVE 'W' CHECK

For one thing, using the Five 'W' Check will ensure that anything we write is kept firmly on track and that we have covered all essential points, eliminating the need for frantic

phone calls and telex messages demanding to know, for example, 'Where?' we would like to have our 100,000 widgets delivered.

Naturally the order of the interrogative group can be changed at will and one or more 'Ws' omitted if they are inappropriate or the answers are self-evident. The important thing is to check off our written communications against our list of 'Ws' to make sure that we have said all we need to say, while incoming correspondence should be checked in the same way so that, if need be, we can respond with a request for more information while the writer still has all the facts to hand. A bonus of the 'W' check is that the winner's own correspondence can be kept short, especially as – taking into account the minimal attention span of many recipients – it's usually best to deal with only one main topic at a time and if possible to cover no more than one side of the paper.

PRACTICAL WINNING

Look through some of your recent correspondence – incoming and outgoing – and ask yourself if it could have been made more effective by checking it against the five 'Ws'. Look for tautology and redundant sentences or paragraphs, as well as unanswered questions, in letters and other writings, bearing in mind that should you find any in this book they are, of course, deliberate mistakes.

ASKING THE IMPORTANT QUESTIONS

The five 'Ws' not only keep our correspondence crisp and to the point but enable us to win with words in many other ways.

'*Who?*', for example, is the question we should ask ourselves before writing a letter, composing a memo, attending a meeting or making a sales presentation. Asking 'Who?' in this way can save time and help us win by establishing exactly who it is that we need to talk or write to. Sometimes it may take several phone calls but it is worth the effort as what we know about the 'who' in question will affect the way we write to them, making it easier to communicate and perhaps helping us avoid a few mistakes.

At the same time, in the case of incoming communications, asking 'who' the people concerned should really be dealing with can often lighten the winner's workload.

'*What?*' is another key question which many people fail to think through before reaching for the phone or dictating a letter.

Everyone wants something, but what exactly is it that *we* want to achieve when we phone, for instance, our bank manager or our lawyer? It's all too easy to have only the main point in mind and to put down the phone before remembering the rest, unless we have a list of 'what' we want with items that can be ticked off as they are discussed.

'*Where?*' is one of the most important questions that winners with words must be able to answer because, now more than ever before, information is power.

Knowing 'where' to find information is virtually the same as having it and avoids the necessity for either an infinitely retentive memory or a filing cabinet the size of the Albert Hall.

As we've already mentioned, winners should have a good comprehensive dictionary; they should also have a modern guide to English usage and a copy of *Roget's Thesaurus* – a series of lists of synonyms and related words. *Roget's* was first published in 1852 and is 'classified and arranged so as to facilitate the expression of ideas.' It has since been brought up to date but it has never been improved upon and if you are lost for the right word this is 'where' to find it. It is also an excellent source of lateral connections that might otherwise wear out a lot of synapses and in this respect is a useful generator of original ideas.

Mind you, the thesaurus, like the dictionary, is addictive and winners should be careful not to get intoxicated by its abundance of words.

Naturally, winners will also have all the specialised reference books they need and will have learned to appreciate the excellent service offered by municipal reference libraries which ensures that in most cases they are only a phone call away from thousands of reference books, together with helpful – and free – assistance in finding what they want.

Reference libraries usually keep file copies of national, regional and local newspapers, together with general interest and business magazines, and there are often business and international reference sections with specialised staff. Winners, of course, will build up their own lists of 'where' to obtain information but the public library is very often the place to start.

PRACTICAL WINNING

Ask yourself if you are getting the most out of your local library and, if not, investigate its reference facilities.

Open a reference notebook for listing any books you find useful, together with titles of any other books you may wish to consult in the future.

'*When?*' always requires precision and it is worth making an extra phone call if you suddenly have a nasty feeling that you have noted down a time or date incorrectly.

Winners try to be punctual; if they are going to be more than a few minutes late they phone ahead to let people know and, while not grovellingly apologetic, they make it clear that their tardiness is not intentional.

Winners don't make too much of a fuss if they are kept waiting for a short while, but once they've gleaned every possible bit of intelligence from the receptionist and the firm's literature they usually find it preferable to make another appointment later in the day.

With outside appointments we always arrange to meet people in places where we would not mind waiting, like a nice warm pub or a hotel lounge – and are amazed by the number of people who apparently enjoy waiting on street corners or on station platforms.

'*Why?*' is one of the most important winning words of all and is a question winners should always ask, not in any cynical way but as a method of control and self-protection.

Why am I doing this? Why do they want me to do that? Why is he asking for that particular thing? Why does she want to go there?

Of course, the majority of these questions will have obvious and satisfactory answers but it is a good thing to acquire the habit of asking 'why?', particularly as it can prevent winners from being swept away by the magic of other people's words.

As an extreme example, in the First World War, asking 'why?' might have saved countless lives, had people demanded to know exactly 'why' they were being asked to sacrifice themselves for a few yards of ground and, more recently, the power of 'why?' was clearly demonstrated when the parents of American teenage youths, and many of the young men themselves, began asking the question about the Vietnam War – and stopped it.

Hopefully none of us will be required to ask ourselves that sort of question but it's clear that, on occasions, simply asking 'why?' could easily save an organisation a great deal of money or prevent its executives from making serious mistakes.

It is as well to ask 'why?' when given an instruction in the workplace that we are not happy about, and winners will be especially on the look-out for answers to 'why' things are done in a particular way which begin with 'Well, we've always done it that way . . .' – an indication that healthy changes for the better could be in order.

'How?' is an honorary 'W' and one to which winners should pay particular attention. We have noted elsewhere that most people like to give advice so winners should be extremely wary of anyone who responds to a question like 'How do I go about carrying out that instruction?' with either a nonchalant 'Oh, you can figure it out' or a blustering 'What do you think we're paying you for?'

To the front-line troops of the workplace it often seems that deciding what should be done is relatively easy, while working out 'how' is the hard part and one in which the winning boss should take a share. If the matter is a really serious one, subordinate winners should make sure they have a written instruction, making it clear that they were told to work out 'how' themselves, although an apologetic smile and a 'Could you let me have a memo on this for my files, please?' will often be enough to make an inconsiderate superior rethink and expand his instructions.

ASKING QUESTIONS – AND ANSWERING THEM

Winners, as we've seen, ask a great many questions and, when they ask them out loud – instead of finding out the answers for themselves in a roundabout way – they are polite and tactful about it.

They also realise that it's very much a losing move to begin to ask a question, either at a meeting or a seminar, and to have to give up half way because they have lost the thread of their argument. This can happen to anyone and the best way to avoid it is to use a version of the Card Trick and carry a couple of blank cards on which to write a few key words of any questions that spring to mind. Winners may never need to use the cards but it's good to know they are there, just in case. Winners ask questions but they also answer questions readily and realise that, if they don't know the answer, the best response is usually 'I don't know, off-hand, but I'll find out and get back to you.'

Children who ask a lot of questions can be a nuisance but they are incipient winners and should be treated accordingly.

Mind you, with children – and often with adults – it's best to find out exactly what the other person wants to know, and there's the salutary story on this topic about the father who answered his small son's query of 'Daddy, where do I come from?' with a long and involved lecture on the facts of life, only to be told in a tone of some surprise, 'That's funny, Tommy comes from Birmingham.'

MUSIC, MUSIC

In winning with words, the question of 'how' we say and write things is often as important as the message and some-times it even is the message. Experts now consider voice quality, for instance, to be so important that the marriage guidance counsellors of Relate now urge couples to take voice tests before they marry, arguing that, when passion cools, living with someone with a high-pitched whine or a booming bellow can put a relationship under real strain.

Of course, not all of us are blessed with vibrant exciting voices of the sort that enable their owners to project confidence, reassurance or sex appeal at will, but even those of us whose vocal cords produce the odd squeak at times, or who have a speech impediment, can be helped or can help themselves. In fact, some people with weird voices or stutters have either made them into trademarks or have been so successful in overcoming them that they have become actors or orators.

One winning move, especially for many women, is consciously to deepen their voice and people can find themselves being regarded completely differently if they are able to deepen their voices even a little. Mind you, an overnight change from a budgerigar chirrup to a Dietrich drawl might cause comment, and even men might find it difficult to explain a sudden change to the bass register, whereas a gradual improvement, combined with a couple of convenient 'sore throats', might not be so noticeable.

One change many people need to make if they are to win with words is to make their delivery more vital and impressive, especially if it is at all monotonous, although in many cases thinking like a winner can be sufficient to effect the required improvement.

Thinking like a winner can change our posture and our breath control which in turn can stimulate the 'kai' force that martial arts experts and practitioners of other strenuous sports call on at the moments of greatest exertion. Winners with words often seem able to harness this mysterious energy, not only to project their voices so that – like actors – they can 'whisper' to the back of the hall, but also to exercise a control over their listeners similar to the spell woven by some types of music.

PRACTICAL WINNING

Ask a partner or colleague to use a cassette to record one of your conversations without you being aware of it – a few minutes ought to be sufficient – and then listen to yourself in private. Even if you have already recorded and listened to yourself reading or making a speech your ordinary speaking voice may come as something of a shock. If your voice sounds monotonous, try speaking the same phrases again, but this time try to vary the pace. Imagine someone whose voice and delivery you admire saying the same things and try to imitate them. Then say the same things in a fake foreign accent – the more atrocious the better – which will not only help you to relax but will prove just how much of a change is possible.

LANGUAGE AND STYLE

Most of us speak what is virtually a different language at home to the one we use in the workplace and many of us are multilingual, using a series of vocabularies and accents depending on the people we are talking to.

Writing styles also vary, but here it is usually a question of choice between informal and formal ways of expressing ourselves.

Speaking – and writing – styles are very much a matter of fashion and styles of expression change as frequently as styles in clothes, so that 'I ain't' or 'it don't signify' are now as quaint as the Dickensian fashions of the people who used them.

Like fashions in clothing, styles of speech and writing can be exaggerated and for those who can bring it off this is often a way of getting themselves noticed. However, there is nothing quite so depressing as last year's high fashion and – although winners should make a point of knowing the up-to-date slang – they should perhaps leave using it to the very young. It is usually preferable to develop a personal middle-of-the-road style which can be varied according to circumstances.

What winners must beware of in both speaking and writing is over-formality, long words and convoluted sentences, all of which proclaim that their user is trying to win with words – and failing.

Winners find that with practice they can change their way, through a sort of communications gearbox in which first gear represents the way they talk and write to their family and special friends, second gear the way they address their colleagues in the workplace, third gear the language of their business talks and correspondence, and fourth gear the ultra-formality of, say, letters of condolence to people who are not intimate friends.

As Randolph Quirk puts it in his introduction to the *Longman Guide to English Usage*, 'Good usage is a matter of combining the rules of grammar and the acceptable meanings of words with an appreciation of our relationship with the addressee.'

PRACTICAL WINNING

Try writing a second copy of your next important business letter, using language closer to that which you use when speaking than your usual written style. Put yourself in the recipient's shoes and ask if the second version might not be more effective than the first. Find a couple of examples of the 'Dear Sir, We are in receipt of yours of the 20th ult, and are at a loss to comprehend . . .' school of business correspondence and translate into something like 'Fred, I've read the letter you wrote on the 20th of last month and I can't understand . . .'

THE RULES OF MAGIC

Grammar is yet another word that has acquired layers of meaning that it doesn't deserve, becoming a word to frighten children and cause many adults, who fear they may not be speaking or writing correctly, agonies of embarrassment.

In fact, those of us who hated grammar lessons at school may well find it difficult to believe that the word – in the form of 'gramarye' or 'gramary' – meant magic, necromancy and occult learning.

Learning 'magic' would have been much more fun than 'parsing and analysing', especially if the children could have been shown how using the magic of grammar could prevent them from making such howlers as 'For sale, desk suitable for lady with bow front and ornate legs.'

Fortunately for those of us whose grammar lessons had nothing of the magical about them, it is possible to learn a great deal of grammar by osmosis, so the winner's interest in well written books, magazines and newspapers will help them pick up most of the grammar they need.

Everything else they need – or want – to know is available in books like the *Guide to English Usage* by Sidney Greenbaum and Janet Whitcut which covers everything from how to use 'a' and 'an' to the spelling and meaning of *Zeitgeist*.

Winners may find that a book of this sort will help them to laugh at the pretensions of people who invariably think they know best – the sort of people, for instance, who say things like 'an hotel' but still pronounce the 'h' or refer disparagingly to 'the' *hoi polloi*. Winners know that using plain words and short, simple sentences will help them to keep their grammar under control. And, after all, the main aim is to be understood – even if we offend those who were taught never to begin a sentence with 'and'.

Grammar, in other words, helps us to make our meaning precise and to avoid errors. Its laws are not immutable and once we have a feel for the right word or phrase it is quite possible to break the rules not only with impunity but to good effect.

WORDS ARE MAGIC – BUT WILL THEY MAKE US RICH?

We've spoken a great deal about the magic of words, the magic of language and how words can help us to win – but win what exactly?

Well, we can't promise that if you are able to win with words you will become a millionaire – although it often seems as though winners with words enjoy a certain material success without trying too hard. This is partly because, while never greedy or money-grabbing, they know how to ask for things like orders, promotions, contracts and help of every kind.

Often they achieve material success simply because they know how to ask, persuade or even order other people to do things, while making them feel like winners – which makes them ideal leaders, team-builders and team-inspirers.

Again, winners with words can use their powers of lateral thinking to produce new ideas, to entertain or to tell stories.

All these are valuable skills but perhaps the most potent magic of words lies in their ability to change their user, both in the short term and the long term, enabling him or her to play their chosen winner's role to the hilt.

Choose your part in life's play; decide *now* whether what you really want is to be a high flyer, a captain of industry, a great lover, a wonderful parent or even a multi-faceted Renaissance Person, and words will help you to achieve and sustain the role.

More importantly, they will help you to be happy in your skin – a real winner in fact – and we couldn't wish anyone better than that.